New York City for Families
5 Boroughs in 7 Days

An Innovative Guide to NYC for the Entire Family

From the Team at RealFamilyTrips.com

Copyright © 2015 by Inspire Conversation LLC.
All rights reserved.

Contact Information at www.RealFamilyTrips.com

This book or any portion thereof may not be reproduced or used in any manner whatsoever without the express written permission of the publisher except for the use of brief quotations in a book review.

Dedicated to our dear children, Noah, Julia, Anna, Sophia, Avery, and Vera. On our continuing journey as a family, we hope to always find new adventures to explore together, even in our own backyard.

All Our Love,

Mommy and Daddy

Table of Contents

Introduction	1
Facts About New York City	4
Why We Wrote This Book	6
How To Best Use This Book:	8
Advice On Enjoying Your Trip:	10
Day 1 - Manhattan, Midtown	12
Day 2 - The Bronx	23
Day 3 - Brooklyn	32
Day 4 - Staten Island	41
Day 5 - Lower Manhattan	56
Day 6 - Queens	70
Day 7 - Manhattan, Midtown	80
Our Hope for You	96
Children's Story: Time Travelling Siblings in NYC	98
Part I	99
Part II	106
Part III	113
Part IV	120
Part V	127
Epilogue	134
Appendix A: Alternate Activities	137
Manhattan	138
The Bronx	171
Brooklyn	177
Staten Island	184
Queens	190

Appendix B: Resources at RealFamilyTrips.com 198
The Team at RealFamilyTrips.com 200
The "Fine Print" 205
Image Credits 206

Introduction

New York City goes by many names - The Big Apple, the City that Never Sleeps, Gotham - all conjure images of a bustling metropolis and a lively city with a lot to offer. Perhaps another name, "The Capital of the World" is even more apt when considering it as a vacation destination.

Few other locations have so much to offer in such little space, boast so many experiences, or touch so many people. New York City definitely tops the list of places that one should see and experience during their lifetime. As much as we can write wonderful things, New York is a city that has to be seen to be believed.

New York City has been at the center of history ever since the new world was discovered and colonized. A center of thought, commerce, industry, and immigration, New York City has served as a leader and set the tone for many other cities. Besides being the center of the New York metropolitan area, the city served as the nation's capital at one time. New York City served as both the last capital under the Articles of Confederation and the first capital under the Constitution. From the founding fathers of the United States of America to the citizens of today, so many people look to New York City for hope and inspiration.

With Ellis Island serving as a onetime gateway to the New World, New York has served as both a literal and figurative jumping off point for the American experience. The coming together of different cultures, beliefs, and ways of life creates a unique melting pot and microcosm of the entire American ideal. This confluence of ideas also breeds the unbridled creativity of some of the world's most cutting edge art, food, technology, and innovation.

In New York City you can walk five blocks and land in a different world than you started in. The city is packed with landmarks and historical sites; from the best known like the Em-Empire State Building and the Statue of Liberty, to obscure slices of Americana and little known delights. New York City truly has something for everyone. Residents can spend their whole live here and barely scratch the surface. If you can't find what you are looking for here, you aren't looking hard enough!

Throughout the years, New York City has been romanticized through art and film, and with good reason. For every example of a great "rags to riches" story in literature or on the big screen, there are many real ones. Fortunes have been made and lives reinvented in New York, a city that has so much to offer residents and visitors alike. The city's energy is palpable and contagious - you may just find yourself walking a little faster or feeling a bit of extra vigor as soon as you hit the streets. Typical New Yorkers have two speeds: fast and faster.

At the same time, for a family visit to New York, the best thing you can do is to throw preconceptions out the window and abandon the idea that there is anything you *must* see or *have to* do. The beauty of New York lies in the abundance of choices, and the fact that there is such a rich and diverse array of experiences to be had. You and your family can tailor the time you spend here to perfectly suit every want and need you have. No matter how varied your tastes are, there is no reason every member of your family, young and old, cannot find something right up their alley in this vibrant metropolis.

When many people think of New York, they simply think of Manhattan. While there is certainly nothing like the island that houses Times Square, Wall Street, Broadway, and much more - all five boroughs offer unique charm and special opportunities for families. From artsy and rejuvenated Brooklyn, to the sweeping green spaces of Queens that allow you to forget you are in the city, to the hidden gems of Staten Island and the diverse landscape of The Bronx - one must experience all areas to truly encapsulate the New York experience.

New York offers so many possibilities within its borders. There are a wide variety of different vacations waiting in the same three hundred or so square miles. Just accept that you will not "see it all" and instead plan to take in the things you truly want to. Savor the time and the experience, and grow together as you travel about.

The choices are yours but the call is simple - visit New York and you just may leave a changed family. Perhaps a new nickname needs to be added to New York City's long list of monikers: The Land of Great Family Vacations.

Facts About New York City

Some Basic Facts About New York City:
- **Population:** 8,491,079 (2014 estimate)
- **Area:** 468.9 square miles total (304.8 square miles land and 164.1 square miles water)
- **Elevation**: 33 feet above sea level
- **Currency:** US Dollar (USD)
- **Time Zone:** US Eastern (EST), UTC-5
- **Counties:** Bronx, Kings (aka Brooklyn), New York (aka Manhattan), Queens, Richmond (aka Staten Island)
- **Settled:** 1624
- **Incorporated:** 1898

Some "Just for Fun" Facts About New York City:

- One of every 300 people in the world lives within 50 miles of Times Square.
- New York City boasts more residents than 39 of the 50 states.
- Someone is born in the city every 4.4 minutes.
- Up to 65% of NYC residents are foreign born or children of parents born abroad.
- New York City has over 500 ethnic groups and over 800 languages are spoken.
- The city is home to 191 colleges and universities and boasts around 950,000 students.
- As of 2007, there were approximately 944,129 business firms incorporated in New York City.
- Central Park is larger than the principality of Monaco.
- The 520 mile coastline of the city is longer than those of Boston, San Francisco, Los Angeles, and Miami combined.
- Every year, over 40,000 location shoots take place in New York City, comprising scenes from films, television shows, commercials, music videos, and documentaries.

Why We Wrote This Book

Why We Wrote This Book is very similar to why we launched RealFamilyTrips.com. Born of the belief that travel is an important part of the family experience, a tool for both growth and fun; it exposes children to new ideas and educates them about the world. It provides opportunities for family bonding that are without compare. By showing your children new people, and ideas, as well as the wealth of history, you harness the past and the present to provide for their future.

We don't believe that "big trips" are something to be put off, or saved until children are "old enough" to appreciate them. Delaying these kinds of opportunities only delays their benefits. Our children surprise us with what they are able to absorb. Of course they may not remember every fact, every site or every detail of a trip when very young, but they will remember how it *feels*. This sensation experienced during great family travel is the part that is really transformative; the power to set a precedent that will follow them throughout their lives. The qualities of worldliness, thoughtfulness, and curiosity are bred in children and nurtured through travel.

As amazing as it is, we also recognize that for a busy family, vacation can seem like anything but, when parents consider the amount of effort, research, and time that go into planning a great getaway. That is why we created Real Family Trips, and why we wrote this book. Our goal is to provide you with a definitive and informative guide, to save you the hassle of planning a trip so you can get on with enjoying it.

We curate days that provide a mixture of what every great vacation needs: opportunities for education, relaxation, excitement, and family time. We select great places, great vendors, and memorable experiences. We place an emphasis on realism, and would never recommend anything we wouldn't personally do, or anything that we know can't realistically be accomplished with several kids in tow.

It is our belief that a great trip requires context and information to accompany it. We encourage you to read sections of this book with your children before departing. Read from the daily introduction while in country, as you make your way from the hotel to your first destination. Emphasize to your children not only what you are seeing, but why. To understand the background, the culture, and the history of what you are seeing and doing is to give it importance and make the most of your experience.

We wrote this book because it is what we would want to have for our family vacations, and now we want to share it with you. We hope you enjoy this trip and those to come in the future. Cherish this time and make the most of your resources. Bon voyage, from our family to yours.

-The Team at RealFamilyTrips.com

How To Best Use This Book:

- The suggested vacation laid out in this book spans 7 touring days in New York City. It is designed so you can start on any day of the week and proceed in order from start to finish.
- This vacation, and the activities chosen for it, **is designed to work any time of year.** While New York City offers unique opportunities in both the warmer months of spring and summer, as well as the chillier months of fall and the cold months of winter, our itinerary in this book is designed to be as universally applicable as possible. There are a few things in both the main itinerary and the alternate activities that are limited by season, but they have been designated as such.
- This trip works from front to back, beginning to end. At the same time, tastes vary. You may have already experienced some of these things in the past or may have different ideas. Appendix A in the back of the book contains some **suggestions for alternate activities**, as well as where they can be most easily swapped in to create a custom built experience for your family.
- All prices are listed in US Dollars and based off estimates from vendors and locations during the summer of 2015. These numbers are intended for informational purposes only, as prices change and may vary based on a variety of factors specific to your family.
- In particular, some museums have family rates and/or annual passes that may be worth looking at for your family. You should look into these online before your trip if possible, as they may also save you time at the ticket counter.

- Similarly, directions to and from locations are based on a "best case scenario" of availability and traffic, and represent average times that are not guaranteed. Buses and subway lines periodically close, and traffic can affect timing greatly. **Beginning and end of day directions are based on the assumption you are staying in Manhattan**, and need to be adjusted if you are staying in one of the other boroughs.
- At the end of each day you will find **two sections labeled "logistics"**: First is a suggested order of the stops for that day. You can change it up if you like; our suggestions are based on ease of transportation and the creation of a cohesive day. Second is a list of clothing, sundries, and other items you may need, or anything else to note and remember.
- We encourage you to read the accompanying children's stories. More about the stories after the main itinerary.
- Finally, Appendix B at the back of the book, provides **additional resources on RealFamilyTrips.com**, including links from us to even more itineraries and ideas for things to do in New York City.

Advice On Enjoying Your Trip:

- Most of the days laid out in this proposed vacation are active and fairly busy. They allow a family to enjoy a wide variety of exciting and educational opportunities. However, if you aren't a "let's pack it all in" kind of family, don't force yourself to follow a plan or itinerary that seems like too much for you. This is likely to backfire.
- Always allow some time for wandering, and you may just discover the unexpected. One day on a past vacation, our family had planned on going on a second hike. We got lost and could not find the trail. As we were about to give up and head back, we rounded the corner and found ourselves by a beautiful glacier-fed lake. Our kids decided to jump into the freezing cold water, clothes and all - we had a blast. This was one of the most memorable and fun parts of the vacation, and it was spontaneous and unplanned. Let those moments happen, and don't stress if something goes amiss with your plans.
- Leave some time to think about and absorb what you saw and experienced, without trying to rush the entire trip. Recap and debrief at the end of the day and during meals. It is absolutely worth sacrificing a stop if it means you have the time to make the other ones really count.
- Push your boundaries and explore things that might be out of your normal character. Immerse yourself in the location. Experience all that the destination has to offer, not just the "main" or "top" tourist sites. Feel what it means to belong there and enjoy the culture and local population.

- Don't follow an itinerary if it simply doesn't interest you. What others think is awesome may be boring to you. No matter how incredible we say the view might be from a boat ride, if you feel uncomfortable on the water then don't do it. Read the planned itinerary and choose what you are interested in seeing. There are also alternate activities in the back (**Appendix A**) which you can mix and match with established plans to make a day that suits you. Don't be afraid to make changes to a plan to make it your own.
- Read the background information for each day and stop with your family to provide context for what you will see. This will help give more meaning to what you experience, prepare you for the trip, and generate excitement. We recommend that you watch movies, film clips, or view other media related to New York City before departing to help prepare and inspire you for the vacation to come.
- Assign projects for the kids. Our kids have to research where we are going. They have been really creative in the past, including drawing a map of our location and identifying the closest Starbucks to our hotel and at each stop we made. The Starbucks was to ensure dad was well caffeinated during the trip. They had fun doing it and presenting it to us, and we had fun listening and seeing what they did.
- Remember the basic things while traveling. Not getting enough sleep or not eating regular meals and snacks can damage even the most well planned trip, especially when children are involved.
- Make sure that you allow extra time, and expect that you will run into some delays. Use these as an opportunity to explore your surroundings and take in the local culture instead of viewing them as a negative.

Have an Awesome Adventure!

Day 1 - Manhattan, Midtown

Manhattan is said by many to be the center of the world, boasting more famous institutions, residents, and events than most other places on Earth. Here you will find the headquarters of the United Nations, the two largest stock exchanges in the world, as well as the headquarters of countless multinational conglomerates that impact our lives on a daily basis.

From the bright lights of Broadway to the cobblestone streets of the Meatpacking District, Manhattan has a world of diversity in a relatively small island. Actually, Manhattan consists of the main island, a few small adjacent islands, and a small neighborhood on the mainland (Marble Hill). Bordered by the Hudson, East, and Harlem rivers, it is the most densely populated county in the United States, also ranking consistently among the densest areas in the world. The sheer number of people and things in Manhattan is astounding.

If Manhattan represents the cultural and economic center of New York, the United States, and perhaps the world, midtown houses more of what we perceive as Manhattan than any other part of the island. Boasting three of the top ten most visited attractions in the world (Times Square, Central Park and Grand Central Station), you and your family can stand at the crossroads of the world and dive head first into the grandeur that is New York City.

This first day in Manhattan offers a chance to set the stage for a grand vacation chock full of great experiences. Set the tone by going big and experiencing education, excitement, and unique locations found only in New York City.

The History of the World - Explore the Museum of Natural History

While New York City hosts a variety of amazing museums (many of which this trip will bring you to) one that stands out, and brings families back time and time again, is the American Museum of Natural History. This museum brings the natural world, as well as the history of man and nature, to life for children. Allow your little ones (or teenagers, who will be equally captivated) to see their history and science books come alive as they stand toe to toe with things they have only read about. Visually this museum is a masterpiece unto itself, the kind of place that puts your jaw on the floor and keeps it there.

From the amazing dinosaur skeletons in the front hall (and throughout the building) to a life sized whale and a comprehensive history of our planet laid out before your eyes, the American Museum of Natural history has it all. This impressive collection is sure to excite the minds and imaginations of the entire family. Depending on specific interests, a variety of special and permanent exhibits may hold the highest appeal. For an additional fee there is a terrific Planetarium, and for another fee there is an IMAX theater. Check out the interactive floor plan to help map out what you plan to visit beforehand and make the most of your time.

Travel Tip: In addition to the floor map, the museum offers a new "Explorer App" - this free mobile application available for iOS and Android, provides turn-by-turn directions "from the edge of the universe to the age of the dinosaurs," plus the shortest route to restrooms, shops, cafes, and exits.

Part of the beauty of this expansive museum is just that - it is huge, thorough, and encompasses an incredible amount of material. You could go every day for a month and still not cover it all. While it may be tempting to spend an entire day here, New York has so much more to offer and time is a premium during vacations. **Here are our recommendations for a few highlights** you can cover in as many hours, making sure you experience the best and still have time to enjoy the rest of your day and more of the city.

1. **David H. Koch Dinosaur Wing** - This favorite section of the 4th floor offers the kind of specimens that are sure to engage any child, as the storied beasts of yore stand before you in full splendor. The wing consists of two separate halls, the Hall of Ornithischian Dinosaurs (Or-nuh-THISH-ee-an) and the Hall of Saurischian Dinosaurs (Sawr-ISH-ee-an). A video explains the difference, and both are more than worth a visit. Full sized skeletons, reassembled and posed next to printed and interactive informational displays, will have you in awe as you stand among giants. Part of the beauty here is that it meets everyone on their level. Older children will learn a lot, while younger children will be amazed, and everyone will walk away with lasting memories.

2. **Milstein Family Hall of Ocean Life** - Explore the most mysterious and diverse climate of our planet today in this hall dedicated to teaching about biodiversity and the evolution of our oceans. This hall goes beyond your average aquarium, sacrificing live animals for the ability to show a collection of model creatures spanning an unprecedented spectrum of ocean life. The highlight and most famous feature is a 94-foot-long, 21,000-pound model of a life sized blue whale. Travel from the frozen arctic to the deepest depths of trenches to see everything from giant squid and sharks, to walruses and penguins. The ability to pair realistic, life sized visuals with the creatures children learn about

in school teaches an invaluable lesson, and leaves an indelible mark.

3. **Discovery Hall** - Those with younger children won't want to miss the Discovery Hall, filled with touchable and interactive exhibits to engage and excite children aged around 2-8 years old. Located on the first floor, this area breaks down natural science to its most basic building blocks and meets children on their own level to provide fun and adventure. Take advantage of this opportunity to ensure that your youngest children get more than just the amazement of seeing a dinosaur or a whale, and also walk away with a bit of information that they can understand. This can help fuel a love for science that will serve them well when you return home. **If your children are older, we recommend devoting more time at the first two stops, or adding a visit to one of the current temporary exhibitions for a slice of something interesting and different.**

These are just our recommendations, to allow you and your family to enjoy some of the highlights in a few hours. If they don't feel like a good fit for you and your children, take a look at the full list of exhibitions and find ideas that work better for you.

Address: Central Park W & 79th St, New York, NY 10024

Phone: (212) 769-5100

Hours: Daily 10 AM - 5:45 PM (Closed Thanksgiving and Christmas)

Website: www.amnh.org/

Approximate Cost: Adults $22, Children 2-12 $12.50, Seniors/Students (with ID) $17.

NOTE: All admissions are suggested. Should you wish or need to pay less, speak with the admissions desk.

Approximate Time: We recommend **2-3 hours**, which is enough time to see the suggested highlights and pack in more during the rest of the day. You choose what works best for your family, but our recommendation is based on personal experience and logistics for the day.

New York's Playground - Walk, Explore, and Grab a Bite in Central Park

Opened in 1857 on 778 acres of city-owned land, this iconic park was later expanded to its current 843 acre size. To put it in perspective, this park sits on approximately 3.5 square miles or about 640 football fields. This is to say, that much like the city itself, this park is *huge*. That size also translates into lots of opportunities for family fun.

In the winter months there is ice skating (See "Trump Rink" in Appendix A for more details) and the chance to play around in the snow or sip on some cocoa. Warmer and temperate months see even more possibilities, with bike rentals and areas to ride, or simply walk, as you explore the area. You can hop into a pedicab or a horse and buggy for a leisurely way to see more of the park without all the work.

There is The Central Park Carousel, originally located in Coney Island and relocated to the park in 1951. This is one of the largest merry-go-rounds in the United States. Central Park is also home to a total of 29 sculptures, most of them depicting famous authors and poets, in an area called Literary Walk. Popular examples include Duke Ellington, Alice in Wonderland, and Balto, the famous sled dog. You might also want to check out Strawberry Fields, the tribute to John Lennon of

Beatles fame. In the summer there is Shakespeare in the Park, as well as concerts and other shows. See the Calendar of Events for more information.

With its history, stunning nature, and many opportunities for activity, culture, and relaxation, Central Park is an oasis within the concrete jungle of New York City and one of its most treasured locales.

Address: Spans from 59th Street to 110th Street, between 5th Avenue and Central Park West (equivalent to 8th Avenue near the park) with multiple entrances.

Phone: (212) 310-6600

Hours: Daily 6 AM - 1 AM (however there isn't much for families to do after dark, and you will want to be cautious about what areas you enter after the sun goes down)

Getting Here: Central Park is located directly across the street (Central Park West) from the Museum of Natural History.

Website: www.centralparknyc.org/

Approximate Cost: Free of charge to enter, some activities cost money.

Approximate Time: We recommend spending about **1-2 hours**

We recommend grabbing a bite to eat in or near the park, where various restaurants, food stalls, and other options exist. Fuel up before continuing your day.

Unique and Hands-On Education - Sony Wonder Technology Lab

Continue your trip south through Manhattan, and arrive at the Sony Wonder Technology Lab, a free, four-story, interactive technology and entertainment museum for all ages. It is not only a great children's museum, it is also a place where creativity is in full bloom.

With more than 14,000 square feet of hands-on interactive exhibit space and over 40 different activities, children and their families can explore the inner workings of electronic devices, create their own animated character, program a robot, perform virtual surgery, and so much more! Check out the complete list of exhibits and let your child pick their favorites.

To complement its permanent exhibits, the Sony Wonder Technology Lab also offers a number of educational programs for all ages. For early learners, *Family Workshops* offer hands-on opportunities for children to learn while using their creativity and fine tuning their dexterity. *Tech for Tots* workshops enable young children and their families to explore technology through fun and interactive activities. *Sci-Tech Workshops* provide grade school-aged children with the opportunity to explore the science of technology, while using their imagination as the main ingredient. You must book ahead and some workshops require a small fee ($10 or less per participant). See the full calendar of events and workshops here.

In addition to its exhibits and innovative programs, the Sony Wonder Technology Lab also offers free movie screenings for children and adults in its High Definition (HD) Theater on Thursday's and Saturday's. See the complete schedule of upcoming screenings.

Free sign language group tours are available on Thursdays at 3 PM. Private sign language tours are also available by reservation, which can be made at least one week in advance of your desired date. Call 212-833-8100 (option 2) to speak with the reservationist.

Travel Tip: While general admission to the Sony Wonder Technology Lab is free, due to its popularity, it's recommended that you call ahead to reserve tickets. Tickets can be reserved up to three months in advance by calling 212-833-8100 (option 2) Tuesday through Friday between 9 AM - 2 PM EST. For those wishing to visit without a reservation, walk up tickets are available on a first-come, first-served basis and can be picked up at the museum entrance. While a limited number of tickets are usually available the day-of, for those travelling to the area planning ahead is key. This high demand destination takes a little foresight to get into, but is well worth it. Call as soon as you have actual dates for your trip.

Address: 550 Madison Avenue at 56th Street New York, NY 10022

Phone: (212) 833-8100

Hours: Tuesday - Saturday 9:30 AM - 5:30 PM, with last museum entrance at 5 PM each day.

Getting Here: About 10-15 minutes either walking or taking a cab from southern points in the park. Varies some with where exactly in the park you are. If you choose to take a subway, use the 4, 5, 6, N or R train to 59th Street and Lexington Avenue / E and M to 5th Avenue / F to 57th Street.

Website: www.sonywondertechlab.com/

Approximate Cost: FREE, however it is recommended you reserve timed tickets.

Approximate Time: We recommend spending about **2 hours** here.

Travel Tip: If you are walking from Central Park to the Sony Wonder Technology Lab, we recommend taking 5th avenue and leaving 20-30 minutes to stop by three great locations on the way:

1. **Apple Store:** The technology giant's New York City flagship store features a 40 foot glass cube in the middle of a plaza, evoking a miniature skyscraper or the Louvre in Paris. Even if you don't go into the 24/7 Apple store, a quick look and photo are sure to be fun.

2. **Trump Tower:** This 68 story structure located at 725 Fifth Avenue is a glittering testament to modern architecture and fixture of one of New York City's most famous streets. Pop in for a visit to the atrium and the stores here, or just admire one of the city's most recognizable buildings.

3. **Niketown:** This five story sporting good emporium is a favorite among kids, with enough merchandise to delight casual browsers and serious "sneakerheads" alike. Design your own shoe, enjoy unique in-store displays, or grab a bit of specialized NYC gear on a stop that has nothing if not some serious "wow factor." **NOTE:** You can access Niketown through the back of the Trump Tower atrium.

End The Day With a Bird's Eye View - Roosevelt Island Tram at Sunset

To round out your day, and cement the variety of experiences available in the city, slow things down with a ride on this historic tram. After learning, playing, and exploring the area around the park, you and your family have had a chance to appreciate the tall buildings from the ground level. Now look down on them from above, with views that will inspire you to continue exploring in the days to come.

The cable car ride, departing from 59th Street and 2nd Avenue, is an often overlooked gem of the New York Experience. The ride is one many New Yorkers have never experienced, which is a shame considering how much it offers for so little. For the price of a good cup of coffee, you'll enjoy hovering over the East River and enjoying sweeping views of Manhattan, Queens, and of course, Roosevelt Island. The large cars hold about 100 people, and are great for spreading out and taking a family photo, or snapping pictures of the scenery.

The tram leaves every 7.5 minutes during rush hour, and every 15 minutes at off-peak hours, meaning you won't have to wait long to get on and enjoy yourselves. If you are just there for the ride, you will have to get off and re-swipe/re-board to ride back to Manhattan, or you can explore Roosevelt Island on foot or through a free bus tour.

If you choose to do a self-guided tour, be sure to check out:

- Southpoint Park
- RIVAA Art Gallery
- North Point Lighthouse
- "The Octagon"

Enjoy your ride and let the rest of today take you wherever it may, then be sure to eat up and get some rest before continuing on tomorrow.

Address: 59th Street and Second Avenue, New York City, NY 10022

Phone: (212) 832 4555

Hours: Sunday - Thursday, 6:00 AM - 2:00 AM. Friday and Saturday, 6:00 AM - 3:30 AM.

Getting Here: Approximately 6 minutes by cab, 15 minutes (1/2 mile) on foot, or 10 minutes by M31 or Q 32 bus from Sony Wonder Technology Lab.

Website: www.rioc.com/#_=_

Approximate Cost: Cost of a single ride (approx. $2.75) is same as a one way fare on a bus or subway, (you can use a MetroCard) or included in an MTA day/week pass. **NOTE - You MUST Pay the Fare Both Ways.**

Approximate Time: About 5-10 minutes ride each way, you can explore Roosevelt Island as long as you like, or head back.

Logistics - Day 1

Suggested Order of Stops:
1. American Museum of Natural History
2. Central Park
3. Stop for Lunch In/Near the Park
4. Walk South and Check Out Apple Store, Trump Tower and Niketown
5. Sony Wonder Technology Lab
6. Roosevelt Island Tram Ride
7. Explore Roosevelt Island

Things to Bring/Note:
- Comfortable shoes for a day with some walking, as well as opportunities for children to run and play in the park/technology lab.
- It is a good idea to invest in a MetroCard to get around. If you plan on using mostly public transit, get one for the week of your visit. If you plan on using it less you might get day passes for days that are more spread out.
- **Be sure to book the Sony Wonder Technology Lab Ahead of Time** and stick to your schedule for access with your timed ticket.

Part I of the accompanying children's stories goes with today's itinerary. We recommend reading the story the night before, or morning of today's journey.

Day 2 - The Bronx

The Bronx is the northernmost of New York City's five boroughs, and the only one located primarily on the mainland. The Bronx is boasts the third highest population density in the country, yet about one quarter of it exists as open land. So while Bronx residents may be packed in tightly, visitors can enjoy the reserved space in the form of a number of parks and destinations, including Van Cortlandt Park, Pelham Bay Park, *the* New York Botanical Garden, *and the* Bronx Zoo.

The Bronx is home to some of New York's greatest artistic and cultural contributions. Art, theatre, music, sports, and more are all alive and well in the borough that houses Yankee Stadium.

For a family vacation, The Bronx offers a chance to spread out and enjoy open spaces, and to see the contrast that exists between boroughs. With some of New York City's best known and most visited attractions, a wealth of history, and opportunities for education - The Bronx teaches families a lot. Perhaps the greatest lesson of all lies in the fact that New York City is alive and well outside of Manhattan.

This second day, spent exploring the storied Bronx, will take you and your family to some of New York City's more famous attractions and a great mixture of activities. Experience nature, wildlife, culture, food, and literature in a single day that shows you just how much of New York there is to see when you venture outside of Manhattan.

A World Class Experience - Visit the Famous Bronx Zoo

The Bronx Zoo, founded in 1899, is the largest Zoo in North America and among the largest in the world. With some 6,000 animals representing over 650 species, the entire world of wildlife is at your fingertips at this New York City landmark.

Conservation and environmental responsibility are at the core of the zoo's mission, with a number of the animals serving as terrific examples of rescue and rehabilitation. As a part of the Wildlife Conservation Society (WCS), the zoo helps to rescue animals and habitats across four continents.

For families, we recommend getting your start on the Wild Asia Monorail. This 1.6 mile ride gives you a great overview, and allows you to see some animals only visible from its windows. Here you'll see tigers, elephants, rhinos, and other native Asian animals, as well as sweeping views of the Bronx River. This wheelchair accessible ride is a great place to start (**PLEASE NOTE**: There is an Additional Fee for this Attraction, unless you buy a "Total Experience Ticket").

After the monorail, some of the highlights of the zoo include:

- **The African Plains Exhibit** - see lions, storks, giraffes, gazelles, and much more, including some of the zoo's most famous animals.
- **Baboon Reserve** - recreates the Ethiopian highlands for a further exploration of the rich treasures of the African wilderness.
- **The Butterfly Garden** - allows you and your children to get up close and personal, as you walk through an indoor butterfly conservatory that takes natural habitats to a new level of interactivity (**NOTE:** Additional Fee Applies if you don't buy a "Total Experience Ticket").
- **Jungle World** - an indoor tropical jungle housing approximately 800 animals ranging from otters, gibbons, and tapir - to beetles and scorpions. Safely observe one of the most extreme climates on the face of the Earth and some of the amazing creatures that call it home (**NOTE:** Additional Fee Applies if you don't buy a "Total Experience Ticket").

Travel Tip: Some exhibits charge admission in addition to the General Admission ticket. All exhibits and attractions are included in the "Total Experience Ticket."

To help decide what matters most to your family, see a full list of activities and programs, as well as a calendar of events to see if something of interest is going on during your visit.

Address: 2300 Southern Blvd, Bronx, NY 10460

Phone: (718) 367-1010

Hours: Spring (April - November) Weekdays, 10 AM - 5 PM. Weekends 10 AM - 5:30 PM.

Winter (November - April) Weekdays, 10 AM - 4 PM. Weekends 10 AM - 4:30 PM.

Getting Here: Approximately 30-40 minutes **by cab** from midtown Manhattan. The BxM11 express **bus** makes stops along Madison Avenue, between 26th and 99th Streets, then travels directly to the Zoo's Bronx River entrance (Gate B). For **subway**, take the 2 or 5 trains towards Wakefield to West Farms Square/East Tremont Ave, walk a third of a mile.

Website: http://bronxzoo.com/

Approximate Cost: (Prices are for "Total Experience Ticket" which allows access to all areas) Adult (13 and up) $30.55 online, $33.95 at gate. Child (3-12) $21.55 online, $23.95 at gate. Children 2 and under FREE. **As you can see, there is a discount if you purchase online.**

Approximate Time: We recommend **2-3 Hours** here in order to maximize opportunities during the rest of the day. You could easily spend an entire day here if you wanted to.

Old New York Culture - Explore and Eat on Arthur Avenue

Here you'll find a unique, small town atmosphere in the middle of the big city. Restaurants that have passed down through generations, mom and pop merchants, and authentic retail locations represent the great-grandchildren of original immigrants keeping the best of the "old country" alive and well.

Arthur Avenue Retail Market is a local fixture and a great place to start. This covered Italian bazaar houses a little bit of everything, compressing the area's butchers, bakers, artisan cheesemakers, and more in one location, to give you an overview of the experience in less time.

Take a little time to poke around and grab a bite before moving on with your day. Just don't forget to say "grazie" (thanks)!

Address: Arthur Ave, Bronx, NY (corner of East 187th Street is a good place to start)

Hours: Hours vary by location, street always available to explore.

Getting Here: Approximately 5-10 minutes **by cab** from the zoo. Alternately, you can choose to walk the half mile, in about 10-15 minutes.

Website: www.arthuravenuebronx.com/

Approximate Cost: Free to walk the area, food varies by location.

Approximate Time: We recommend **about 1 hour** here to keep things moving.

A Jewel of the City - Tour the New York Botanical Garden

Spanning some 250 acres of the Bronx, this designated preservation area represents some of the greatest natural beauty one can find in all of New York City. While areas like Central Park offer fun, casual relaxation, and recreation, the Botanical Garden is an educational experience of carefully manicured gardens and curated exhibitions.

Once upon a time the land was used for commercial purposes, but it was acquired by New York City in the late 19th century to create a space for nature advocacy and a living museum of plants and landscaping. The collection of gardens includes both indigenous and imported plant collections, and the grounds also house extensive research facilities and archives.

Regular plant and flower shows shine a spotlight on some of the most prized collections, and present the impressive "collections" in a way that is very engaging for children. In late winter and early spring the Orchid Show is a local favorite, amassing incredible collections of the delicate flowers for a visual feast. The annual holiday Train Show (which typically runs from mid-November through mid-January) creates incredible replicas of New York City landmarks out of plant materials, surrounding them with festive model trains for a wonderful experience for children, teens, and adults alike. Another frequently used motif is to combine famous works of art combined with re-creations of the landscapes depicted in them, with past shows featuring artists such as Monet and Frida Kahlo. See the calendar of events and exhibitions to see what is coming up at the gardens.

While some children may be hesitant about the excitement factor of visiting a garden, most are quickly won over at this facility that sees plant life as a spectacle. The New York Botanical Garden is far more than just an idyllic open space in the middle of The Bronx, it features plants on the same majestic scale as the surrounding buildings, resulting in a quintessentially "New York" version of a garden experience.

Address: 2900 Southern Blvd, Bronx, NY 10458

Phone: (718) 817-8700

Hours: Tuesday - Sunday, 10 AM - 6 PM (January - February closes at 5 PM). Closed Mondays, except certain holidays.

Getting Here: Located directly north of the Bronx Zoo. Approximately 5-10 minutes **by cab** from Arthur Avenue. The 1.6 mile walk would take about a half hour, or you can a Bx12 or Bx22 **bus** in about a half hour.

Website: www.nybg.org/

Approximate Cost: Weekdays - Adults $20, Children 2-12 $8, Children under 2 FREE. Weekends and Holiday Mondays - Adults $25, Children 2-12 $10, Children under 2 FREE.

Approximate Time: We recommend **2 hours** or so, in order to get a feel and get in one more stop after.

Literature Comes Alive - Visit the Edgar Allan Poe Cottage

This small cottage, located in the eponymous Poe Park, is where the literary giant spent the last years of his life, from 1846 to 1849. It was here that he penned some of his most famous works, including "Annabel Lee," "The Bells," and "Eureka."

In Poe's time, the cottage offered unobstructed views of the undeveloped hills and vistas of The Bronx that extended as far as Long Island. Today, with the surrounding area built up and commercialized, it offers a curious glimpse of a simpler time. See this quaint wooden farmhouse built at the turn of the 19th century off the bustling Grand Concourse and marvel at the dichotomy, admire New York City's storied past and pay tribute to one of America's great writers.

The guided tour, led by guide Neil Ralley, offers a wealth of information about Edgar Allen Poe and the time that he lived. Enjoy a film presentation, and authentic period furnishings that enhance the scene. Complete with dishes on the kitchen table, one gets the feeling that if they turn their head; the great author himself might be standing there, wondering how you got into his home.

The adjacent park offers an opportunity to stretch out and let the kids run themselves down at the end of the day, as you reflect on great adventures and plot your next great experience.

Address: 2640 Grand Concourse, Fordham, Bronx, NY, 10458

Phone: (718) 881 8900

Hours: Saturday, 10 AM - 4 PM. Sunday, 1 PM - 5 PM. Thursdays and Fridays 10 AM - 3 PM. Other weekdays by prior arrangement only.

Getting Here: Approximately 10 minutes **by cab** from the Botanical Garden. You can **walk** the 1 mile in about 20 minutes, or take a Bx22 **bus** towards Bedford and arrive in about a half hour.

Website: www.bronxhistoricalsociety.org/poecottage.html

Approximate Cost: $5 for Adults, $3 for Children.

Approximate Time: About **1 hour**, maybe less. The tour is short, but you can relax in the park longer if you like.

At this point, wrap up your day by grabbing dinner in the area, or heading back towards your lodging to eat and rest up for tomorrow's fun.

Logistics - Day 2

Suggested Order of Stops:
1. Bronx Zoo
2. Walk and Eat on Arthur Avenue
3. New York Botanical Garden
4. Edgar Allan Poe Cottage

Things to Bring/Note:
- Comfortable shoes for a day with a fair amount of walking.
- This day in the Bronx may be easier to accomplish by taking cabs, though if you do plan on taking buses, a MetroCard will help.

Part II of the accompanying children's stories goes with today's itinerary. We recommend reading the story the night before, or morning of today's journey.

Day 3 - Brooklyn

Brooklyn is New York City's most populous borough, and perhaps the one that has transformed the most in recent years. With widespread gentrification and an explosion of business, art, food, and culture, Brooklyn is quickly growing to rival Manhattan as a destination.

Active children will enjoy the storied past of Brooklyn as a center for sports and recreation, with the recent acquisition of the Brooklyn Nets *cementing a legacy of sport from a borough that has produced such greats as* Vince Lombardi, Joe Torre, *and* Michael Jordan. *The* Brooklyn Academy of Music *has long stood as a testament to the influence of music on and by the borough, while the* Coney Island Mermaid Parade *and* Nathan's Hot Dog Eating Contest *establish it as a center for fun and frivolity.*

Part of the beauty of Brooklyn, as with all of New York City, is in its diversity and the enclaves of culture that allow you to seemingly traverse entire continents in a few blocks. The world is at your fingertips as you experience the landscape of Brooklyn.

For your third day in New York City, delve into Brooklyn and explore all that it has to offer. Enjoy great views and some hands-on opportunities to explore history, while also taking a break to enjoy some good old fashioned family fun. The mixture of education and recreation will be a welcome change of pace in the trip, as well as a great encapsulation of the Brooklyn experience.

Time for Some Fun - Visit and Play at Coney Island

Educating and exploring other cultures is an important part of any family vacation, but any great trip also needs to allow time to cut loose and enjoy some good old fashioned fun. Use this morning to blow off some steam and enjoy the sights, sounds, and excitement of Coney Island, a great amusement center in the heart of the city.

Coney Island came into popularity in the late 19th century, as a playground for the rich. From around 1880 to the end of World War II, the area was one of the most popular amusement centers in the country. Rides, shows, beaches, and more attracted visitors from all over New York City, and the country at large. After the war, the area fell out of popularity and was largely neglected, as the old roller coasters rusted and the bright lights faded.

In recent years, a resurgence in both interest and investment have brought about a sort of renaissance here. In this way, Coney Island serves as a microcosm for the whole of Brooklyn; with what was old becoming new again and a surge in popularity fueling new growth, with more attitude and offerings than ever.

There is so much to do here, and your choices will depend on your family. Stroll the boardwalk and indulge in some snacks, games, and shopping. Hit the beach for some fun in the sun, and swim, sunbathe, or run around to your heart's content. Enjoy some fun rides and classic amusements. Not the amusement type? Take in a fantastic aquarium and enjoy sea life on the sea side. Then again, you can always choose not to choose, and simply take in a little bit of everything!

Interested in special offerings like the The Mermaid Parade, Ask The Experts Lecture Series, and other special events? See a calendar of upcoming events around the time of your trip online.

Travel Tip: Only a handful of Coney Island's attractions have websites and other contact information. Your best bet is to simply get there and play it by ear, but if you are the type that likes a more definite plan, we have included website and/or phone info for attractions whenever possible.

Some top attractions and destinations at Coney Island include:

- Luna Park, Scream Zone & The Cyclone Roller Coaster - (718) 373-5862
- The New York Aquarium at Coney Island - (718) 265-3474
- MCU Park and the Brooklyn Cyclones - (718) 449-849
- Deno's Wonder Wheel Park - (718) 372-2592
- Eldorado Bumper Cars and Arcade - (718) 946-6642
- Abe Stark Rink - (718) 946-6536
- Nathan's Famous - (718) 333-2202, 1310 Surf Ave. & 1129 Boardwalk

Summer Tip: Fireworks shows take place at 9:30 PM every Friday night during the season (last weekend in June, until and including the Friday before Labor Day). If you would like, wind your way back here at the end of the day to enjoy the show!

PLEASE NOTE: Coney Island is an arts and entertainment district/neighborhood, not a centrally located or managed amusement park like you may be accustomed to. Individual attractions have different ownership, hours, contact information, prices, and policies which vary greatly.

Address: Surf Ave. Brooklyn NY 11224

Hours: Vary greatly by location. Rides and attractions operate seasonally, generally from about Easter - Halloween. The beach and boardwalk are open year-round (though there are only lifeguards Memorial Day - Labor Day). The New York Aquarium is open almost every day of the year.

Getting Here: Express **bus** from Manhattan, X28, X38. By **train**, take the D, Q, N or F train to Stillwell Avenue. This takes about 45 - 60 minutes from midtown Manhattan.

Website: www.coneyisland.com/

Approximate Cost: Free to explore, amusements and food vary by location.

Approximate Time: We advise spending **2-3 hour**s here to start the day, enjoying your morning before moving on.

We recommend grabbing a bite to eat on the tail end of your visit here, as you fuel up for a busy rest of the day that involves some walking.

Just For Kids (But Fun For Adults Too) - Brooklyn Children's Museum

Tucked away in the heart of Brooklyn, lies a true gem of a family destination. This children's museum was the first of its kind in the United States, and some say the world. Founded in 1899, the original directors saw the need to reach out to children and offer educational opportunities that not only conveyed knowledge, but a sense of fun and excitement about learning. We couldn't agree more!

Back when the museum was founded, its primary purpose was to expose urban children to natural science, but over the years the museum has expanded to cover a wide variety of material. Today, technology and culture are a major part of the offerings, and ever since the museum's founding, children have actually been involved in the planning of exhibits to ensure the creation of engaging material that opens minds from a young age.

Travel Tip: During the summer months, the museum offers free admission hours on Thursdays from 2 PM - 6 PM.

Permanent Exhibits include:

- **Totally Tots** - Sensory exhibits for 0 - 5 year olds which include sand, water, music, and more.
- **Neighborhood Nature** - Explore life science and nature from native Brooklyn and learn more about the surrounding area.
- **World Brooklyn** - Miniaturized shops that mimic those of Brooklyn neighborhoods aid in an exploration of culture. Provide your family a chance to gain insight into the unique institutions and people that make Brooklyn great.
- *You can also check the* Calendar *for a list of visiting exhibits and special events.*

Address: 145 Brooklyn Ave, Brooklyn, NY 11213

Phone: (718) 735-4400

Hours: Tuesday - Sunday, 10 AM - 5 PM. Closed Mondays.

Getting Here: Approximately 30 minutes by **cab** from Coney Island. 1 hour by **train**, take the Q or B to the 3.

Website: www.brooklynkids.org/

Approximate Cost: $9 per person, Children 12 months and under FREE.

Approximate Time: We advise spending about **2 hours** here before moving on.

Walk Through History - Self-Guided Tour of Cobble Hill

This tree-lined, historic district of Brooklyn hasn't changed much over the years - and that is a good thing. As much of the surrounding area develops and gentrifies, Cobble Hill retains old world charm with quaint brownstones lining narrow streets and winding alleys.

On Henry Street, south of Kane Street you'll find the house that Winston Churchill's mother Jeanette was born and raised in (though some people dispute this, so to be safe, walk Amity Street near Court Street where others claim she grew up). Carroll Park, located between Court, Smith, Union, and President Streets, has a famous World War I memorial dating back to 1921).

This neighborhood contains a number of charming shops, cafes, patisseries and boulangeries - as well as a healthy stock of upscale retail establishments.

Take your time as you wander as much of the 40 or so blocks here as you like. Take time to pop in a shop or two, grab a snack or a drink, and take in the delightful architecture as you enjoy a glimpse into Brooklyn's past.

Address: Start near Court Street and Kane Street, Brooklyn, NY.

Getting Here: Approximately 20 minutes by **cab** from Children's Museum. 30 minutes by **train**, take the C to Jay Street or the 3 to Borough Hall.

Approximate Time: We advise spending about **1 hour** here wandering, less if kids start to get tired.

Take in the View - Walk Brooklyn Heights Promenade

Also known as "The Esplanade", this scenic vista is one of the best views in the city. Wind down your day in Brooklyn looking out over Manhattan and the surrounding area, enjoying another spot perfect for a breath of fresh air and some calm amidst the clamor of the city streets.

This 1,800 foot walkway is maintained by the New York City Parks Department. It is visited by countless tourists every year, and has been a staple of film and television for its idyllic setting and sweeping views. Its length also makes it a great stroll for a family, no matter how young your children are, as you don't have to commit to a long walk to really get a lot out of your time. The promenade is also lined with benches and a few playgrounds if either a little rest, or a little more activity, are needed to keep the children happy.

Besides being a beloved tourist stop and a fixture of media and culture, the site has played host to a bit of history. The nearby Brooklyn Heights neighborhood is where Dutch settlers first established the settlement of "Breuckelen" in 1645. It was from this spot that George Washington watched the Battle of Brooklyn unfold, and Robert Fulton captained The Clermont on its maiden voyage up the Hudson River.

Enjoy your time strolling and admiring the view, and be sure to take plenty of pictures. This will be one of the best photo opportunities of the entire trip, and watching the sunset from this outlook will be something to remember.

Address: Montague St & Pierrepoint Pl, Brooklyn, NY 11201

Phone: (718) 722-3214

Hours: This walkway is always available, though you are in for a special treat if you time this stop around sunset.

Getting Here: 5-10 minutes by **cab** from Cobble Hill. You can also take a **train** in about 20 minutes, opting for the F to York Street or the 3 to Clark Street.

Website: www.nycgovparks.org/parks/brooklyn-heights-promenade/map

Approximate Time: We advise spending **a half an hour to an hour** here just to get a flavor for it and enjoy the view.

Indulge in Local Fare - Grab Dinner in the Area

To wind down your day in Brooklyn, we recommend taking the time to seek out some local fare and enjoy a leisurely dinner. This day, which started at the southernmost points in the borough, has brought you back almost all the way to the Brooklyn Bridge, and close to Manhattan once again. With a quick cab or subway separating you from the end of your day, take some time to explore the area and find a place that appeals to you.

As we have tried to stress, Brooklyn is a true melting pot of cultures, and it really shows in their culinary offerings. You can find nearly any cuisine you can imagine (and some you might never have thought of) sprinkled throughout most neighborhoods.

Logistics - Day 3

Suggested Order of Stops:
1. Coney Island
2. Brooklyn Children's Museum
3. Historic Cobble Hill
4. Brooklyn Heights Promenade
5. Grab a Bite in the Area

Things to Bring/Note:
- Comfortable shoes for a day with some walking.
- If you think you might want to spend time at the beach while at Coney Island, be sure to bring bathing suits, sunscreen, towels, and a change of clothes for after.
- Seeing as Brooklyn is easily accessible by subway, a MetroCard will help if you do plan to avail yourselves of public transportation.

Part III of the accompanying children's stories goes with today's itinerary. We recommend reading the story the night before, or morning of today's journey.

Day 4 - Staten Island

Staten Island is the least populous borough of New York City and is often overlooked, especially by tourists. This is a shame, considering how much the area has to offer families, with a variety of kid-friendly activities to rival other areas of New York City.

The southernmost of New York City's boroughs, Staten Island enjoys views of Brooklyn, southern Manhattan and New Jersey. The north of the island is the most urbanized area, featuring historic neighborhoods and gorgeous Victorian homes. The western side is the least developed and home to heavy industry, while the beaches of the east are very popular and feature the two and a half mile F.D.R. Boardwalk, the fourth-longest in the world.

The residential neighborhoods of Staten Island offer a relatively quiet setting, while still being marked by the same history and richness of culture that all of New York enjoys.

It is worth a day trip to enjoy the hidden gems and lesser known attractions of Staten Island. While most people fail to look past Manhattan, show your family a slice of real New York City life that is very worth the trip.

Your fourth day will start with some of the scenic views that lend perspective and generate excitement, before you dive into some of the best of Staten Island. Enjoy art, history, and culture that even many locals manage to overlook, with a day that opens your eyes in more ways than one.

A Famous Ride - Trip on the Staten Island Ferry

The Staten Island Ferry has been a vessel for both efficiency and recreation, serving commuters and tourists alike, since 1817. It is the only publicly operated transport that was more expensive back in 1948, when it cost a dime to ride, as the now free ferry ride offers some of New York City's best views to anyone who chooses to take the five mile ride.

Set sail from the southern tip of Manhattan, crossing New York Bay, and enjoy stunning views of Ellis Island and the Statue of Liberty. The ride is just long enough to savor your surroundings, while still keeping up a brisk pace for you to enjoy the day. The ferry departs every 30 minutes or so (every 15-20 minutes during rush hour), and operates 24/7.

The ferry has come a long way since the origins of New York City. In the 1700s, ferry service was provided by private individuals with small twin mast sailboats called peraugers. Eventually, the city took over the route and established public ferries, solid boats which even attracted the U.S. Navy to purchase three of the vessels from New York to put into service during the Civil War.

Travel Tip: The Staten Island Ferry terminals and several of the ships (currently the F/B Spirit of America and The F/B Andrew J. Barberi) have free WiFi. Soon all the ships in the fleet will offer this service.

Be sure to snap some photos during your trip, both of the views and the family set against the backdrop, as you all get excited for your upcoming adventure on Staten Island.

Address: Manhattan - Whitehall Terminal, 4 Whitehall Street New York NY 10004

Staten Island - St. George Terminal, 1 Bay Street Staten Island NY 10301

Phone: Inside NYC, dial 311 for information. Outside NYC, call (212) NEW-YORK.

Hours: 24/7, every 15 - 20 minutes during rush hour, every 30 minutes off-peak.

Getting Here: If taking a train from points north in Manhattan, take the 1 to South Ferry Station, the 4 or the 5 to Bowling Green, the J or the Z to Broad Street or the R to Whitehall Street.

Website: www.siferry.com/

Approximate Cost: FREE of charge.

Approximate Time: About **1/2 hour** each way.

The Island's Most Idyllic Setting - Explore Snug Harbor Cultural Center

Also known as "Sailor's Snug Harbor," or just "Snug Harbor," this botanical garden and cultural center is a lot of things rolled into one great destination. This location encompasses educational opportunities spanning history, art, architecture, theater, dance, music, *and* environmental science, which come together in a unique and exciting way.

This one time home for retired sailors is actually a campus of 26 repurposed buildings, 6 of which were the very first to be designated as landmarks by New York City's Landmark Preservation Commission in 1965. Add to that 9 separate and distinct botanical gardens, a two acre urban farm, and 10 acres of wetlands - all set on a campus totaling 83 acres in the heart of Staten Island - and you have one interesting facility.

The **Visual Arts Center** features a contemporary art gallery, a selection of rotating exhibits, and support for artists in residence. See cutting edge presentations and support the New

York City art scene through fun and affordable galleries that meet children on their level and are more family friendly than some of the larger venues in Manhattan.

Heritage Farm is a working farm that operates on sustainable principles and provides quality food to the community, while maintaining a focus on education. Learn about agricultural techniques, sustainable practices, and the importance of eating locally. Who knows, a visit here might just have your kids more excited about eating their vegetables!

The **Horticulture** section features 9 separate gardens, each with a separate focus and different offerings (more on one of them below).

Check the calendar for **Upcoming Events** and see what kinds of activities coincide with your trip. Many are free, and others very affordable. This facility is focused on community service rather than profit, and it is a great place to see a lot while saving the sting associated with many of New York City's major tourist destinations.

Travel Tip: There is also a children's museum located on the grounds of Snug Harbor, the Staten Island Children's Museum. You can easily include it in your time here, opt for it over the gardens and art exhibits, or omit it entirely, depending on your preference. More about The Children's Museum below.

While at Snug Harbor, we feel no visit is complete without a stop at the Chinese Scholar's Garden.

The garden is included with all the horticulture exhibits, $5 for adults and FREE for 12 and under.

This unique locale within Snug Harbor provides a slice of life in ancient China, and an oasis of calm amid the busy borough. Based on Ming Dynasty (1368-1644) gardens, the facility was crafted by a team of 40 Chinese artists and craftsmen who spent a year in China researching and creating, followed by another 6 months on Staten Island assembling the facility. It is one of only two authentic scholar's gardens in the United States. Experience the type of setting that inspired the art and literature of Confucian, Buddhist, and Taoist monks, as well as other scholars throughout history.

Explore eight pavilions, a bamboo forest, waterfalls, a Koi-filled pond, Chinese calligraphy, and a 15-foot rock formation.

Enjoy whatever you like at Snug Harbor, as you settle on a combination of art and outdoor activities to appeal to your family.

Address: 1000 Richmond Terrace, Staten Island, NY 10301

Phone: (718) 425-3504

Hours: Tuesday - Sunday, 10 AM - 5 PM.

Getting Here: About 6 minutes by **cab**, or 15 minutes by **bus** S40/S44 or S90/S94 to Richmond Terrace/Lafayette Avenue.

Website: http://snug-harbor.org/

Approximate Cost: Gallery OR Garden, $5 for Adults and FREE for children 12 and under. Combo ticket for both is $8 for Adults, FREE for 12 and under.

Approximate Time: We recommend spending **1-2 hours** here to keep things moving for the rest of the day.

Fun for Younger Kids - Staten Island Children's Museum

PLEASE NOTE: Based on personal experience, we feel the children's museum is best suited for ages 6 and under. Ages 7-9 will enjoy some exhibits, while children older than 9 may want to pass on it. **This facility is located on the grounds of Snug Harbor**.

On the campus of beautiful Snug Harbor, which offers art, gardens, and more for families - lies a Staten Island institution since 1976. From the large metal sculpture, Francis the Praying Mantis, that greets you as you enter (created by Lenny Prince of Lenny's Creations - a visit to Lenny's Creations is described below), to the friendly staff and hands-on exhibits, The Staten Island Children's Museum is a warm environment dedicated to interactive learning.

The museum's mission statement indicates a dedication to "nurture the creativity and curiosity natural to all children, to recognize and celebrate different learning styles, and to demonstrate vividly that learning can be exciting and fun." For very young children, it accomplishes just that. It presents a number of interactive exhibits that spark interest and imagination, getting children ready for more practical learning when they return home. While it may not hold the same appeal to older siblings, part of the beauty is that the location in Snug Harbor makes it possible for your family to split up, with some enjoying the kiddie fun here, while older children and/or a parent explore the surrounding gardens and other attractions.

Current exhibits at the museum include:

- House About It - use the digger and the wrecking ball, work with a real drill, design and decorate an unfinished home as you learn about building.
- Bugs and Other Insects - wear a bug's exoskeleton and crawl through a human-sized ant hill.
- Walk-In Workshop - Wednesdays and Thursdays from 1:30 - 4:30 PM, weekends from 1 - 4 PM, and Thursdays from 11 AM - 1 PM (for tots) enjoy arts and crafts.

- Great Explorations - learn about extreme environments, explore the rainforest canopy, journey to the ocean floor, and ride a dogsled.
- Block Harbor - build, play, explore, and enjoy this kiddie pirate ship full of games.
- Sea of Boats - this outdoor, soft surface play-space features a lighthouse, crow's nest, and more that offer chances to jump and climb as children learn about Morse code, fishing, and radar.
- Ladder 11 - children can ring the bell, slide down the pole, hook up the hose and try on the clothes as they pretend to be firemen and women while learning about the life-saving pursuit.
- Portia's Playhouse - this real stage does double duty. Sometimes it is a space with costumes perfect for thespian-themed pretend time. At other times, it is an actual performance space for children's shows.
- Garden Terrace - learn about plants and nature, and enjoy an opportunity to enjoy a nature-themed play area outdoors.
- Big Games - enjoy chess with child-sized pieces, giant dominoes, bowling, checkers, connect four, and more in this area dedicated to larger-than-life fun.

Download a floor plan from their website to prepare for your trip, and check out the calendar for upcoming events.

Travel Tip: Visit at the end of a Wednesday during the summer to enjoy "Boogie Woogie Wednesdays." These include FREE admission at 5 PM, snacks at 6, and dancing/activity from 7-8.

This museum has fun areas that encourage children to cut loose. There are also good opportunities for parents and children to enjoy activities together. Play a game, plant something, or watch the daily animal feeding together and make sure your New York City vacation includes time for kids to be kids and blow off some steam.

Address: 1000 Richmond Terrace, Staten Island, NY 10301 (Located on the grounds of Snug Harbor)

Phone: (718) 273-2060

Hours: Tuesday - Saturday, 12 PM - 5 PM (opens at 10 AM during summer). Saturday and Sunday 10 AM - 5 PM. Closed Mondays.

Website: http://sichildrensmuseum.org/

Approximate Cost: $6 per person, ages 1 and up.

Approximate Length: We recommend spending **an hour** here.

Unique Urban Art - Take a Look at Lenny's Creations

For something really different, experience the artwork of Lenny Prince, an auto mechanic with a love for classic cars, bold statements, and big pieces. His original artwork is made up almost entirely of scrap metal, using junked cars to create incredible animals, robots, vehicles, panoramas, and so much more. Some tower over you, reaching heights as tall as 10 feet!

Travel Tip: You can get tickets as soon as you arrive on Staten Island, at the cultural lounge of the ferry terminal.

The pieces are large, innovative, and sure to impress everyone in the family, from young children to teenagers that have "seen it all." This is simply one of those charming, "only in New York" type exhibits that support a local artist and gives you a chance to step into something different. Enjoy over 100 original works of art in this relatively small space. There is also a good chance you'll get to meet the man himself, as Lenny Prince enjoys seeing how his work is received by the general public.

FUN FACT: You may already be more familiar with Lenny's work than you know. There is a good chance you just saw his giant sculpture of a praying mantis outside of the Children's Museum of Staten Island, located on the grounds of Snug Harbor.

If you really enjoy the work, there are small sculptures for $12-$15 dollars that can make for memorable souvenirs of a unique stop on your New York adventure.

Address: 16 Rector St, Staten Island, NY 10310

Phone: (718) 759-7344

Hours: Saturday and Sunday, 11 AM - 8 PM. If interested in visiting on a weekday, call ahead and see if they can accommodate you. Either way, we recommend calling ahead (even on weekends) to ensure it is open.

Getting Here: About 5 minutes by **cab**, or 10 minutes by **bus** S40 to Richmond Terrace/Clove Road.

Website: www.lennyscreation.com/

Approximate Cost: $5 per person.

Approximate Time: We recommend about **a half hour** here. It is a small facility and you should be able to see it all in that time.

Explore the Past - Explore Historic Richmond Town

Right in the center of Staten Island, you'll find a living piece of history in the Richmondtown neighborhood. This key seat of power throughout the history of Staten Island housed settlers of primarily Dutch, English, and French descent during the colonial era, followed by a garrison for British troops during the American Revolution.

The modern facility houses over 30 buildings, spanning the late 17th to the early 20th century. Here they pay homage to the colonial era people who lived in the area, working primarily as craftsmen and tradespeople, such as blacksmiths and cobblers. The agriculture of the community is recognized by several farmsteads and nearby Decker Farm, which offers a seasonal farm stand and annual activities such as pumpkin picking in the fall. There are also buildings of historical significance to local government, including the Third County Courthouse.

Founded in 1958 with cooperation from the Staten Island Historical Society, the current facility spans 25 acres and includes 15 restored buildings families can visit and tour. Experience a 300 year old colonial village complete with historical reenactors, offering a unique slice of life from days past.

Travel Tip: Every Friday is FREE admission day, save money and get the same great educational opportunity.

The experience mimics that of other historical towns like Colonial Williamsburg, with the added benefit of enjoying such a quaint setting just blocks from a modern urban center. This quiet oasis and historical enclave in the middle of Staten Island is a great way to juxtapose "then" with "now" and show children how far New York City has come.

Fun Activity: Find the "Britton Cottage" in Historic Richmond Town to help your trip come full circle. This former home of Nathaniel Lord Britton, founder of the New York Botanical Garden, will help you better understand and appreciate what you saw on Day 2 in The Bronx (and read in the Day 2 story).

This large facility contains more artifacts and exhibits than we could mention here. The guided tours are the best way to get an overview of the facility and learn context as well as some interesting historical tidbits from the knowledgeable staff. Check out the calendar of events and programs to see if there is a special outing that may interest you (tickets available online two *weekdays* before each event).

Address: 441 Clarke Ave, Staten Island, NY 10306

Phone: (718) 351-1611

Hours: Wednesday - Sunday, 1 PM- 5 PM, Closed Monday and Tuesday.

Getting Here: About 20 minutes by **cab**, or 30-40 minutes by **bus** S54 to Arthur Kill Road/Cemetery 1 Gate.

Website: www.historicrichmondtown.org/

Approximate Cost: Adults $8, Children 12-17 $6, Children 4-11 $5, Children Under 4 FREE.

Approximate Time: We recommend about **1 - 2 hours** here.

For the evening, we have two options for activities. Choose what works best for your family based on tastes, and seasonal availability.

Option 1 - New York City Baseball with the Staten Island Yankees

The quintessential American pastime is alive and well in New York City, and while taking in a game with the Yankees or Mets is great, families might just have more fun with the relaxed atmosphere of a minor league game. The Staten Island Yankees are a farm team for their major league counterpart of the same name, and children will delight in the opportunity to see future stars and other up and comers in a small town setting.

The single A team plays games in a smaller stadium, which means you and your family are closer to the action. Less expensive ticket prices also make it an affordable option, as you will drop under $20 a person and get the whole family in for less than the cost of a single major league ticket. The historic stadium offers stunning views of lower Manhattan, Brooklyn, and New Jersey as you take some time to get off your feet and let the fun and excitement come to you.

Travel Tip: Even though the stadium is small and walkable, try to grab tickets along the first base line if you can. These seats offer some of the best skyline views to enjoy between innings, the opportunity for a chance at a foul ball, and a quick in and out to get you back to your accommodations at the end of the game.

Like most minor league games, the baseball is just part of the fun. You and the kids will enjoy great entertainment and activities between innings, and if you check the schedule you might just have a chance to enjoy one of the fun and festive theme nights, replete with costumes, giveaways, and more! All Friday and Saturday night games include a fireworks show after the game. Enjoy a chance to bond under the lights of a riveting night game, and enjoy local fun in a classic American setting.

Address: 75 Richmond Terrace Staten Island, NY 10301

Phone: (718) 720-9265

Hours: See Schedule for listing of games. Evening games are typically at 7 PM, while Sunday games are at 4 PM. Season runs from June - September.

Getting Here: About 30 minutes by **cab** from Historic Richmond Town, or 45 minutes by **bus** S74 to Bay Street/Borough Plaza. Conveniently located next to the Staten Island Ferry for your return trip.

Website: www.SIYanks.com/

Approximate Cost: 3 levels of ticketing, $9/$15/$18 per person, depending on where you want to sit.

Approximate Time: Game length varies, stay as long as you like as this is your last stop.

Option 2 - Walk or Cycle Fort Wadsworth

Fort Wadsworth, on the east coast of Staten Island, is one of the oldest military sites in the United States, as well as a gorgeous open area of Staten Island to explore with your children. The fort protected New York City for over 200 years, taking advantage of its location to cover The Narrows (the tidal strait between Brooklyn and Staten Island) now spanned by the Verrazano Bridge. Working with the Brooklyn based Fort Hamilton, this fort created a crossfire that deterred potential enemies from making their way into the Upper Bay area and accessing Manhattan. A crucial player in both the Revolutionary and Civil Wars, when the fort finally closed in 1994, it was the longest serving garrison in the United States.

Today the fort is part of the 26,000 acre Gateway National Park, which spans 4 counties, 3 boroughs, and two states. You can tour the historic fort and delve into its rich military history. Alternately, if you feel like winding down the day with a more casual stop, rent some bikes and cycle the area, or take a leisurely stroll to admire the sights. See New York Harbor from the same vantage point of the men and women who defended it during colonial times, and enjoy spots that let you view ancient battlements and towering modern high rises from the same place.

Address: 210 New York Avenue Staten Island, New York 10305

Phone: (718) 354-4606

Hours: The gateway is open year round, generally from sunrise to sunset. Specific buildings may only be open seasonally or on weekends, and may have abbreviated hours. However, the surrounding area for walking/cycling is always accessible.

Getting Here: About 20 minutes by **cab** from Historic Richmond Town, or 45 minutes by **bus** S74 to Midland Avenue/Richmond Road and a transfer to the S51 to Battery Road/Tennessee Road (though for simplicity, we recommend a cab for this leg).

Website: www.nps.gov/gate/learn/historyculture/fort-wadsworth.htm

Approximate Cost: FREE to visit, charge applies if you choose to rent bikes.

Approximate Time: Stay as long as you like as this is your last stop, though there will be less to see and do once the sun goes down.

End the Day - Travel Back to Manhattan

After a day full of activity, it is time to return to your accommodations and rest up for your next adventure. We recommend ending your day the same way you began it, with a ride back on the Staten Island Ferry. The view will be quite different at night, and afford you and your family a chance to admire the lights of lower Manhattan as you approach.

Staten Island Ferry - St. George Terminal, 1 Bay Street Staten Island NY 10301

From the Staten Island Yankee game it is a 5 minute **cab** ride back to the ferry, a 5 minute **bus** ride on the S44 towards St. George Ferry to the Richmond Terrace Stop/Schuyler Street, or you can opt to **walk** the fifth of a mile along Richmond Terrace in about 5-10 minutes.

From Fort Wadsworth it is a 15 minute **cab** ride to the ferry station, or about 25 minutes by **bus** on an S51 towards St. George Ferry to the Bay Street/Borough Plaza stop.

You can also opt to take a cab all the way back to Manhattan if you are feeling particularly tired, be advised that the trip

back to midtown can be pricey and may take about 45 minutes to an hour.

Logistics - Day 4

Suggested Order of Stops:
1. Staten Island Ferry Ride
2. Snug Harbor Cultural Center (Including Chinese Scholar's Garden)
3. (If Travelling With Younger Kids) Staten Island Children's Museum (Located on the Grounds of Snug Harbor)
4. Lenny's Creations
5. Historic Richmond Town
6. Staten Island Yankees Game (If In-Season) **- OR -** Walk/Cycle Fort Wadsworth
7. Travel Back to Manhattan, by Ferry if Possible

Things to Bring/Note:
- Comfortable walking shoes for a day with ground to cover.
- There are lots of great photo opportunities on this day, so be sure to bring your phone or camera.
- **If You Plan to See a Baseball Game, Best to Purchase Tickets Ahead of Time** and bring them with you.

Day 5 - Lower Manhattan

Returning to the bustling streets of Manhattan, join the 56 million annual tourists who know that this relatively tiny island is a place where dreams are made and education comes to life. While midtown is currently the busiest part of the city and the epicenter of commerce and culture, New York City was actually founded at the southern tip of the island and gradually expanded northward. The **Castello Plan**, an early map of the Dutch colony of New Amsterdam from 1660, shows the tiny settlement in the days of muddy streets and little centralized government. At that time, **Wall Street** was an actual wall, built to protect the tiny southern tip of the island and its handful of settlers from incursion originating in the wilds above.

As the settlement expanded and more of Manhattan became built up, the lower part of the island remained a center of commerce and government. New York City Hall lies in the southern part of the island, between Broadway, Park Row, and Chambers Street, and is the oldest city hall in the United States that still houses its original governmental functions. Wall Street has gone on to become a center of the financial world, and the **World Financial Center** (also known as Brookfield Place) houses some of the most significant financial institutions of the New York Stock Exchange and NASDAQ index.

Today, lower Manhattan house such important and exciting neighborhoods as Tribeca, Chinatown, Little Italy, SoHo, Nolita, Chelsea, the Lower East Side, The Financial District, The Meatpacking District, Five Points, and Alphabet City. Each has unique things to offer and a breadth of history and culture packed into a central area.

This fifth day will take you from the very bottom of the island upwards, spanning sites of historic significance and chances for family fun.

The View From the Bottom - Breakfast and Sightseeing in Battery Park

Start your day at the very bottom of the island of Manhattan, enjoying the same views (with a *very* different skyline) as the original settlers. Battery Park is a relatively small preserved area, which draws its name from the battery of artillery that once stood there to protect the surrounding settlement. It was the setting for Evacuation Day celebrations, which marked the departure of the last British troops following the end of the American Revolutionary War.

Today, the park offers an opportunity to enjoy unobstructed views from the edge of Manhattan, with no buildings to stand between you and New York Harbor. You can choose to enjoy the gardens, or see if there is an event coinciding with your visit, but we recommend keeping it short.

Some of the real value here is in the pristine vistas that afford a great chance to view the Statue of Liberty and Ellis Island in all their glory. The statue, a gift from the French, was dedicated in 1886. Made of copper (whose natural patina has given it the signature green hue) stands over 150 feet tall and weighs over 200 tons. Its position in New York Harbor has served as a symbol of freedom and democracy as it has gained an international reputation and become synonymous with the city which displays it.

Ellis Island served as a historical center for immigration, as the nation's busiest inspection station from 1892 until 1954. It was here that millions of soon-to-be-Americans first set ground on their new nation's soil, and began their journey to search out the American dream.

While both The Statue of Liberty and Ellis Island are important and fascinating visits (find more information in Appendix A at the back of this book), because they are located on islands, visiting these sites means sacrificing a lot of touring time to get to them. We recommend taking this opportunity to view them and discuss their significance with your children as you eat some breakfast in the park, before starting a day that will allow you to see a lot more by staying on the mainland. Of course, each family is different and visiting one (or both) of these places may be important to you. Discuss with your children, and if you decide you do want to visit, swap something else out to allow time to make the trip.

Address: Located between Battery Place and State Street

Hours: The park is always open, and we advise getting an early start today to pack in as much as possible.

Getting Here: If taking the **subway,** the 4/5 stops at Bowling Green, the R stops at Whitehall Street and the 1 stops at the South Ferry station.

Website: www.thebattery.org/

Approximate Cost: FREE to visit, there are a variety of food options nearby for any budget.

Approximate Time: We recommend spending a **half hour** or so here before moving on to get the most out of your day.

The Original New Yorkers - National Museum of the American Indian

An exploration of the history of both Manhattan and New York City as a whole wouldn't be complete without a recognition of its first settlers, the Native Americans.

Located in the Alexander Hamilton U.S. Custom House, the building itself is a national historic landmark and a stunning example of classic New York architecture. Valencia-born engineer Raphael Guastavino designed the elliptical rotunda with its 140-ton dome skylight, and the building features majestic marble columns and murals from world renowned artists. A special tour allows you to see The Collector's Office, with Tiffany Studio designed woodwork, not normally accessible to the public.

While the architecture is amazing, we recommend spending your time on one of the 45 minute -1 hour tours that center on the exhibits. See ceramics from Central America that include amazing works of gold, jade, stone, shell, and more. The Glittering World tour and exhibit highlights Navajo jewelry as a form of symbolism and cultural identity. Infinity of Nations takes a look at a variety of peoples and cultures from North, South and Central America, showing cultural exchange and the connectedness of native peoples even before the arrival of European settlers.

Insider Tours offer an in-depth look at certain aspects of Native American life, ranging from beading, music makers, and textiles, to native games. Led by a "cultural interpreter" from the museum, you and your family can really dive into a given subject on this carefully curated tour of relevant artifacts within the museum. See the calendar to help plan your visit, or reach out by email (NMAI-NY@si.edu) to make arrangements for your family.

Address: Broadway, New York, NY 10274 (Between Bridge Street and Bowling Green)

Phone: (212) 514-3700

Hours: Daily, 10 AM - 5 PM, Open until 8 PM on Thursdays.

Getting Here: Easiest to simply walk the 10th of a mile (1 1/2 blocks) east on Bridge Street and North on Broadway. One way streets actually mean you need to circle around in a **cab**, turning the two minute walk into a 5 minute ride.

Website: www.nmai.si.edu/

Approximate Cost: FREE of charge.

Approximate Time: We recommend spending **1-2 hours** here.

Financial Education - Walk and Explore Wall Street

Wall Street may not be large, spanning 8 blocks and about 3/4 of a mile across lower Manhattan, but the amount of wealth, history, and power that reside here are impressive. Home to the New York Stock Exchange and NASDAQ, the two largest stock exchanges in the world, this street has become synonymous with the institutions that reside here, and the heart of one of the most impactful financial districts in the world.

Once upon a time, Wall Street was an actual wall, serving to protect the settlers of a burgeoning Dutch colony from incursion from the north. Over time, the city expanded and the area took on new significance. A buttonwood tree that stood at the foot of the street in the 18th century became a gathering place for speculators to come together and trade securities. The consolidation and formalization of their efforts took the form of the Buttonwood Agreement in 1792, which afforded certain standards and protections to traders, and laid the groundwork for the future stock exchange. Besides this longstanding status as a financial center, Wall Street was also the site of George Washington's inauguration as President of the United States, further cementing it as a place of national importance.

Some quick highlights for your self-guided walking tour should include the New York Stock Exchange, the Federal Reserve (underground, it houses a gold vault containing over $100 billion in bullion), and famous Trinity Church.

Getting Here: You can take a 5 minute **cab**, an uptown 5 **train** for about 5 minutes, or if you are up for it, walk the third of a mile in about 10 minutes, following Beaver Street northeast.

Approximate Cost: FREE to explore on your own.

Approximate Time: We recommend spending about **a half hour** here exploring.

A Maritime Retreat - Lunch and Tour at South Street Seaport

The first pier of this historic seaport made its debut in 1625, as an early outpost of the Dutch West India Company. Since then, this area between Fulton Street and the East River served as a center of industry and shipping that connected the "New World" to the countries that colonized it. With shipping and the import/export business forming such an integral part of the early days of New York City, this location provides an important piece of the puzzle as you explore the origins of Manhattan and the ever developing significance of the area on both the national and world stages.

Now a designated historic district, here you will find the largest collection of restored early 19th-century commercial buildings in the entire city. This commercial center/museum setting includes original mercantile buildings, renovated historical ships, the former Fulton Fish Market, and a modern mall featuring food, shopping, and activities for families.

The South Street Seaport Museum offers a Visitor Center at Schermerhorn Row with FREE admission to the lobby area, which features rotating displays and activities for children. The Street of Ships allows you to board the lightship *Ambrose* or the barque *Peking*, as well as the chance to get on a chartered sail in the East River during the spring and summer. The Bowne Print Shops and Maritime Crafts Center on Water

Street offers family activities that explore letterpress techniques from the 19th century and an explanation of local trades from the past.

If any of these locations are of particular interest to you, we encourage you to carve out more time for a longer stop. For most families, your best bet is to take in the free information at the visitor center and do some exploring on your own to see some of the historical buildings and admire the ships. Follow this up with a light lunch at one of the many local eateries, and move on to continue your day.

Address: 19 Fulton St, New York, NY 10038

Hours: Monday - Saturday, 10 AM - 9 PM. Sunday, 11 AM - 9 PM.

Getting Here: About 5 minutes from Wall Street by **cab**. You can choose to take the 2 **train** one stop to Fulton Street in 5-10 minutes, or **walk** the third of a mile, taking Water Street northeast to Fulton Street.

Website: www.southstreetseaport.com/

Approximate Cost: FREE to visit, food varies depending on where/what you choose.

Approximate Time: We recommend spending about an **hour and a half** or so here, including lunch and exploration time.

Powerful and Important History - Visit the National September 11th Memorial/Ground Zero

PLEASE NOTE: This stop is most appropriate for children who are able to deal with the heavy subject matter. If you believe your children can handle it, we think this is a very important stop to make.

September 11th, 2001 was a day that rocked the world, and that those who lived through will never forget. The horrifying attack on the World Trade Center and Pentagon was a tragedy that resulted in almost 3,000 deaths, yet also produced many stories of heroism and personal sacrifice.

The site is a powerful experience and an emotional visit. To remember a time when the world's eyes turned to New York City, it helps us to honor those who lost their lives and those who worked so hard to protect their fellow man. It also reminds us of the indomitable spirit of New York, as the city stood tall and refused to live in fear.

Located at Ground Zero, and the former footprint of the Twin Towers, this national memorial and museum tells the story of that infamous day, as well as the heroes who helped to make rescue and recovery possible. A forest of trees, with two massive pools that stand in the footprints of the fallen towers, serve as a powerful visual and a sobering reminder to punctuate your vacation with some of the most important history of the modern age.

The corresponding museum features 23,000 images, 10,300 artifacts, Over 500 hours of video, and nearly 2,000 oral histories of the fallen, provided by friends and families. These poignant exhibits help convey a sense of the human impact of the attacks, and lend faces and names to the fallen in a unique and fitting way.

Travel Tip: Tickets are distributed by date and time, with ticketing available 3 months in advance. Due to the incredible popularity of this site, we recommend booking online as soon as you have exact dates for your trip to make sure you get in at the time you want. **Museum Tickets include the 9/11 Memorial.**

Considering the devastating nature of the material here, we advise setting aside time to speak with your kids and share your own stories from this terrible day. Help them to understand what it was like to actually live through, and use this tragic time as an opportunity for a powerful discussion and chance to bond as a family.

Address: 180 Greenwich St, New York, NY 10007

Phone: (212) 266-5211

Email: reservations@911memorial.org

Hours: Daily, 9 AM - 8 PM.

Getting Here: About 5-10 minutes from the Seaport by **cab**. About 20 minutes by **bus,** taking a free downtown connection towards Battery Park City, getting off at South End and Albany Street.

Website: www.911memorial.org/

Approximate Cost: Adults $24, Children (7-17) $15, Children 6 and under FREE. We recommend that you book online.

Approximate Time: We recommend spending about an **hour** or so here.

Chic Shopping and a Beautiful Walk - Explore SoHo

While Fifth Avenue is the first to pop into everyone's minds when it comes to high class shopping and fashion, the hip neighborhood of SoHo houses some of the city's best food and poshest retail outlets. Standing for **So**uth of **Ho**uston, SoHo is a neighborhood on the rise, only (fairly) recently having gone from cheap digs to one of the city's most desirable ZIP codes.

The area's unique and charming aesthetic is defined by preeminent examples of cast-iron architectural elements, as well as the Belgian blocks that pave many narrow sidestreets. This creates a smaller-city feel that some describe as more European than the high rises of midtown.

SoHo's history has been marked by a number of dramatic shifts in makeup and purpose. As Broadway and the theater district expanded, along with major hotels and upscale shopping, it drove the middle class southward. Between 1860 and 1865, nearly 25% of the residents were driven out of the area, replaced by small manufacturing concerns and tradespeople to service the theater and other industries to the north. Over time, the city center continued to migrate north, with manufacturing moving further south, or off Manhattan completely. With SoHo lying between two worlds, largely unoccupied former warehouses and similarly large spaces lay empty. This led to a new population of artists, attracted to the huge windows and natural light afforded by former mills and factory spaces, and cheap rents made possible by quickly abandoned buildings.

The artistic flair continued to flourish in SoHo, gradually evolving into a center for everything hip, young, and fashionable. Today SoHo stands as one of the most fashion-centric neighborhoods in New York City, with world class boutiques and major international chains populating the now very in-demand real estate.

Travel Tip: Shopping in SoHo is hard to beat, but also far from cheap. If your family is on a budget, enjoy shopping the windows of SoHo and make your way down to Canal Street. On Canal you will find many more affordable options, as well as some souvenir-type purchases for great prices.

Besides the fantastic shopping opportunities, be on the lookout for these fun SoHo attractions:

- **Subway Map** at 110 Greene Street, between Prince and Spring. Created by Belgian artist Francoise Schein in 1986, this "Subway Map Floating on a New York Sidewalk" consists of metal rods embedded in the concrete, serving as a functional piece of art you can walk on.
- **Art Galleries** still have a strong presence in SoHo, harkening back to the roots of the neighborhood's gentrification and emergence as a cultural force. Even if you aren't "in the market", you and your family can enjoy some great works of cutting edge art for free by popping in for a quick look.
- **The Mercer Hotel** is worth a visit, even if you don't choose to stay here. Built in 1890 for John Jacob Astor II, the six-story, square brick building has been cited by the New York City Landmarks Preservation Commission for its perfect example of Romanesque Revival architecture.

Address: Located Between Houston and Canal Streets, 6th Avenue and Crosby Street.

Getting Here: About 10-15 minutes from Ground Zero by **cab**. If you choose the **train**, take an uptown 1, A, C or E to Canal Street for a trip lasting about 15-20 minutes.

Approximate Time: We recommend spending about **one to two hours** exploring, depending on how much the shopping aspect interests you.

Wind Down in Bohemia - Dinner and Fun in Greenwich Village

Known to locals as simply "The Village", this is another one of those New York City neighborhoods that you have to *feel* and experience for yourself to truly understand. Here you'll depart from the big chain stores and find an eclectic and charming mix of small, specialty vendors selling everything from old books to delicious chocolates. Take in local flair and find a number of "only in New York" venues and attractions.

Originally comprised of farmland for the Native Americans and later, colonials, who settled here, Greenwich Village gets the "village" part of its name from the fact that it originally developed as a separate municipal entity. Until 1829, it served as a bucolic retreat from the rapidly expanding city that surrounded it, a sort of suburb within the city proper.

After incorporation into the city, The Village became known for the artistic flair and progressive thinking of its residents. It has long served as a center for original thought, and has stood on the cutting edge of art and culture as a focal point of new movements and ideas. Politics, art, music, and literature all owe much to this neighborhood, a sort of incubator for the cutting edge, from the Beat Movement of the 60's to the birth of jazz and folk music.

This spirit of intellectual development is encapsulated by New York University's current dominance of the neighborhood. This quintessential city school is a great sight for those with soon-to-be college bound teens, and the surrounding area has a lot to offer in the way of art, theater, dance, comedy, poetry, music, and more.

Take some time to explore together and find a place that appeals to you to stop for dinner. Along the way you might find a place to check out a small show, hear some music, or do a little more shopping.

Some Things to See in Greenwich Village:

- **Grove Court**, on Grove Street is the setting for O'Henry's famous short story, "The Last Leaf" and a beautiful little courtyard in front of an interesting building, visible from the street.
- **Washington Square Park** in the heart of NYU territory is a bustling center from which to see a variety of different people and maybe catch a street performance or two.

- **The Bitter End** at 147 Bleecker Street is a legendary rock club that helped launch the careers of such greats as Joan Baez and Bob Dylan. It is worth walking by to see that they are still running strong. **Note**: Not for young kids, age minimum to enter varies with show.
- **The Comedy Cellar** at 117 Macdougal Street isn't the place to visit with your kids, but walking by you might just catch a glimpse of someone you know from TV as some of the nation's top comics make regular appearances. **Note**: The club is 21 and older to see a show.
- **The Blue Note** is a legendary jazz club that has been on the scene for many years, making its home at 131 W 3rd Street. **Note**: This is one of the more kid friendly music venues in the area, and table seating is all ages. There is a $5 food/drink minimum for all visitors.
- **Cafe Wha?** located at 115 Macdougal Street is a high energy music venue and former hangout of Jimi Hendrix, Allen Ginsberg, and many others. Visit after dinner. Not a great idea for younger kids, but might be a fun choice for older kids, for whom a drink minimum is replaced by a $20 food minimum. **Note**: The music is great, but very loud, which may bother some children.

Address: The neighborhood spans from 14th Street down to Houston Street, reaching from the western edge of the island to Broadway.

Getting Here: You can simply wander north of Houston on foot, or if you like, take a 1, 2, or 3 **train** north to Christopher Street, or an A, C or E north to West 4th Street to start in the heart of the neighborhood.

Approximate Time: Keep going as long as you still have energy left. This is the last stop of your day and can be as long or as short as you like.

Logistics - Day 5

Suggested Order of Stops:
1. Battery Park and Breakfast
2. National Museum of the American Indian
3. Walk Wall Street
4. Lunch and Tour at South Street Seaport
5. National September 11th Memorial
6. Walk and Shop SoHo
7. Wander/Dinner In Greenwich Village

Things to Bring/Note:
- Comfortable shoes for a day with some walking.
- Manhattan is so easily navigated by public transportation, that a MetroCard makes the most sense and will really help you get around quickly and easily.
- **Decide in advance** if you plan to visit the National September 11th Memorial/Museum. Both because you should arrange tickets in advance, and because if you choose to **omit it**, you can spend more time at the South Street Seaport or the later stop in SoHo.

Part IV of the accompanying children's stories goes with today's itinerary. We recommend reading the story the night before, or morning of today's journey.

Day 6 - Queens

Queens is New York City's largest and easternmost borough. The vast expanses of Queens are decidedly "New York" while shedding some of the steel and concrete superstructures for greener areas and quaint homes. While there are parts of Queens that have a definite urban quality, including the neighborhoods of Astoria and Flushing - there are also neighborhoods like Bayside and Little Neck, that make it appear as if you have left the city for the suburbs.

Queens holds a selection of landmarks and industries as diverse as its neighborhoods. Here you will find the two airports servicing New York City, JFK International and LaGuardia, creating some of the busiest air traffic in the world. However, mere miles away, you will also find Rockaway Park beach, Aqueduct Racetrack, and Flushing Meadows Park - which serves as home to the Mets as well as the US Open.

While often passed over by tourists, the diversity of Queens offers numerous opportunities for both traditional and practical education. Immersing yourselves in the borough for the day allows you to enjoy one of the most culturally diverse areas in the world, while taking in unique museums, parks, and an array of food and retail outlets.

The second to last day of the trip will allow you to enjoy some fascinating and informative museums, as well as some downtime in the sunny green space of the borough's less urban areas.

Rural Charm in an Urban Setting - Visit Queens County Farm Museum

Queens County Farm museum is where the past meets the present, and the city meets the country. This 47-acre parcel represents the largest remaining undisturbed tract of farmland in New York City, and the longest continuously farmed site in New York State.

With a history dating back to 1697, the facility maintains an historic farmhouse (dated 1772) as well as planting fields, greenhouses, a historic orchard, herb garden, apiary, and children's garden. See farm machines and implements from days of old on through the modern age, and view how farmers work the land today, carrying on the 300+ years of agrarian history at the site.

Perhaps most germane to families, particularly those with younger children, are the working farm animals. See sheep, cattle, goats, pigs, hens, and honeybees up close and personal (maybe not *too* close for the bees!) and enjoy a nice change of pace for your family.

Travel Tip: Visit the welcome center to receive a farm map with animal locations and purchase goat feed, for a chance to interact with the animals. You can choose to walk the grounds yourself, taking in the fields, the animals, the equipment, and more.

If you visit on the weekends, stop by the Adriance Farmhouse. Free, guided tours are available on Saturdays and Sundays from 11 AM - 4 PM (on the half hour) for families and individuals. Hayrides are also offered on Saturdays and Sundays only, weather permitting (11 AM - 4 PM, April-October), for $3/person.

This tranquil retreat from the hectic city will be a nice change of pace. For those used to urban settings, who live in the area, or have simply adjusted over the early days of your trip - it is a literal breath of fresh air and a welcome bit of variety.

Address: 73-50 Little Neck Pkwy, Floral Park (Queens), NY 11004

Phone: (718) 347-3276

Email: info@queensfarm.org

Hours: Daily, 10 AM - 5 PM (open year-round).

Getting Here: Coming from Manhattan, it could take about 45 minutes to an hour by **cab**. Considering the expense of this proposition, we advise taking a QM5 **bus** towards Glen Oaks to Little Neck Parkway/260th Street. This could take about an hour and 15 minutes, but seeing as the museum doesn't open until 10 AM, it still makes sense. You will spend your day working back towards Manhattan, making the return trip easier.

Website: www.queensfarm.org/

Approximate Cost: General Admission is FREE, <u>unless</u> there is a special event going on. You can likely still get in, but may have to pay for the event. See the calendar to double check your date. Groups and organizations should call in advance to make a reservation, and admission fees apply.

Approximate Time: We advise spending **1-2 hours** here to keep the day moving.

A Slice of the Jazz Life - The Louis Armstrong House Museum

Louis Armstrong was one of the greatest musicians of his day, or any day for that matter. With a name that became synonymous with Jazz, the trumpet player was an international sensation, prominent African American, and a beloved personality who crossed lines and helped break barriers both musically and socially.

As the museum itself is quick to point out, Louis' international acclaim meant he could have lived anywhere, and his choice to settle in Corona, Queens speaks to the quality of the neighborhood and the classic New York spirit of the man. This house, purchased by Armstrong and his wife Lucille in 1943, was where they lived until the end of his life. Lucille donated the home to the city to serve as a museum, and the furnishings remain the same as they were during their residence here.

The immersive experience of the museum takes you inside a "day in the life" of Louis Armstrong and his wife, as tour guides take you through the home. Hear private audio recordings that go beyond just exposing you to the music. You and your family get a chance to "practice" with Louis, listen to him share a meal with his wife, and talk with friends - all while standing in the very places the recordings were taken. This unique take on the life of a great artist is insightful and shares a lot of information on the man himself, his legacy, and the importance of jazz music.

From the down-home feel of the living room, to the personal flair of the Japanese style garden, this tiny museum packs a lot of enjoyment and helps you show your children a different side of city living.

Address: 34-56 107th St, Corona, NY 11368

Phone: (718) 478-8274

Hours: Tuesday - Friday, 10 AM - 5 PM. Saturday and Sunday, 12 PM - 5 PM. Closed Mondays.

Getting Here: About 20 minutes from the farm by **cab.** Alternately, you can take a Q46 **bus** to Queens Boulevard, connecting to an F **train** to Jackson Heights, then a 7 train to Corona Plaza. This complicated route takes about an hour and a half, so we advise springing for the cab here.

Website: www.louisarmstronghouse.org/

Approximate Cost: Adults, $10. Children $7, but under 4 are FREE.

Approximate Time: The guided tour lasts about **45 minutes** and then you will have to leave.

A Welcome Break - Lunch, Relax, and Play in Flushing Meadows - Corona Park

Time to take a break from a day full of immersive and educational opportunities for a little fun in the sun and a quick (or long, if you really need the break) bite to fuel up for the rest of the day.

Flushing Meadows Corona Park is famous as a retreat for New Yorkers and a setting for great events. It was here that two separate World's Fairs took place during the twentieth century, and you can still see remnants in the form of the famous "Unisphere", an internationally known sculpture from the 1964/1965 fair. This 12-story, spherical steel globe was dedicated to "Man's Achievements on a Shrinking Globe in an

Expanding Universe." It also makes for a great family photo opportunity!

The largest park in Queens, Flushing Meadows Corona Park offers a wide variety of activities and facilities. There is the massive recreation complex, as well as plenty of open green space to spread out or run around, depending on your particular needs. Interested in doing something a bit more? The park offers several fun options:

- **Flushing Meadows Corona Park Golf Center**: Walk down the Passarelle Ramp from Willets Point Station to enjoy some great mini golf to break up the day.
- **Willow Lake:** Offers opportunities for canoeing/kayaking, as well as paddle boats for a nice mix of active and relaxing activities on the water. Don't want to actually get wet? Consider some fishing.
- **Sports:** Those who want to work up a little sweat, children who want to get in some practice during the off-season, or families who just like to play a game together can find fields and facilities for basketball, soccer, baseball, tennis, biking, ice skating (outdoors in-season, when rink is not being used for events), and volleyball.

- **Playgrounds:** Are great for younger children, or if mom and dad need a little break to just sit and watch. See the guide to their locations in the park.
- Not the active types? Need to check in with work? See the park guide to Wi-Fi Hot Spots and just kick back.

Do as much or as little as you like here, and be sure to check the park guide to available eateries to grab that bite before moving on. Alternately, you could step outside the park and find a local restaurant if that better suits your family (Just don't wander TOO far, because your last stop for the day is located in the park).

Address: Grand Central Parkway, Whitestone Expressway between 111 Street and College Point Boulevard, Park Drive East

Phone: (718) 760-6565

Hours: Certain areas are open 24/7; others have operating hours which vary by activity.

Getting Here: About 5-10 minutes from the Louis Armstrong House by **cab.** Alternately, you can take a Q48 **bus** towards Flushing Main Street to Roosevelt Avenue. This option takes about 15-20 minutes.

Website: www.nycgovparks.org/parks/flushing-meadows-corona-park

Approximate Cost: FREE to enjoy the park, food varies by location.

Approximate Time: Play it by ear and do what makes you happy, but we advise **less than two hours** of activities here in order to fully enjoy the next stop, though you won't have to travel for it.

One More Great Museum - Explore the New York Hall of Science

Founded in 1964 as part of the 1964/65 World's Fair, this hands-on science museum has gone through an incredible change. One of the only facilities from the fair to remain open after the fair's end, the museum later closed for almost 10 years. During that time, it shifted its focus from science fiction to practical lessons in biology, chemistry, and physics.

With over 450 permanent exhibits, and a regular rotation of exciting featured displays, workshops, and events, the hall is the only hands-on science and technology center in New York City. This facility was *made* for families (the material is geared towards ages 1-17), and allows your children to get excited about the world around them through a host of displays that let you touch, play, and immerse yourselves in the subject matter.

Travel Tip: The museum has FREE admission hours on Tuesdays from 2 PM - 5 PM, and Sundays from 10 AM - 11 AM.

The museum is all about having fun while you learn. Some highlights include soap bubble making, the interactive TVs of "Connections: The Nature of Networks", arts and crafts areas, a hall of mirrors, and the leafcutter ant farm. If you need to take a break and cut loose, play some mini golf (**NOTE: this costs an additional $5 per child**) or enjoy an outdoor, science themed playground (with an indoor play area in case the weather is bad). You may also choose to slow things down, and take in a show at the 3D theater.

To plan your visit, we recommend downloading a copy of their map. Share it with your children so that they can pick their favorites, and use it as an opportunity to get them excited about their trip and about science.

You should also check the calendar, to see if any special events or programs coincide with your visit, and what special exhibits are on at the time.

Address: 47-01 111th St, Corona, NY 11368

Phone: (718) 699-0005

Hours: Weekdays, 9:30 AM - 5 PM. Weekends, 10 AM - 6 PM.

Getting Here: The Hall of Science is actually located inside the park, so wind down your time there by making your way to the western edge, where the museum is located.

Website: http://nysci.org/

Approximate Cost: Adults, $15. Children (2-17) and Students, $12. You can purchase tickets online before your visit.

Approximate Time: We advise leaving at least **2 hours** for this stop, but as it is the last of the day, stay as long as you like before returning.

Getting Back - Return to Manhattan

Getting back to Manhattan will be easier and quicker than the morning's journey to the far end of Queens. You can opt for a 30 minute **cab**, or take a 45 minute journey on the 7 **train** towards Times Square, arriving at midtown and easily connecting to wherever you need to get from there.

Logistics - Day 6

Suggested Order of Stops:
1. Queens County Farm Museum
2. Louis Armstrong House Museum
3. Flushing Meadows - Corona Park (Relax/Play, Eat)
4. New York Hall of Science

Things to Bring/Note:
- Comfortable shoes for a day with some walking.
- Plan ahead for your time in the park and dress accordingly. Loose, sporty clothing for running around, a bathing suit for canoeing, or whatever you think you might need for your chosen activities.
- Queens can be trickier to navigate than other boroughs. A MetroCard will be a big help to get to and from Queens at the beginning/end of the day, while cabs make more sense in the middle.

Day 7 - Manhattan, Midtown

Having gotten a taste for all five boroughs of New York City, and having experienced the glorious diversity they have to offer, it is time to come back to where it all began for you and your family. Midtown Manhattan is the beating heart of the city, with more people, sights, and activities per square block than anyplace else. Take advantage of that fact and see it once more, with the context gained from your six days touring the far corners of New York City.

Midtown has come a long way since its days as the center of the carriage trade, with the horses giving way to the bright lights most commonly associated with the big city. This is the place where locals come to work and everyone comes to play, with a healthy mix of the unique and the "touristy" that allows someone in the know to experience it all.

Embrace the spirit of New York City you have been building up throughout your trip, and see some of its most important sights. Also take advantage of this final day to pick up any last minute gifts, take a few more great pictures, and share in a few more experiences. Round out your view of New York City and your amazing family vacation the same way - by sharing them together.

This last day of the trip combines a few "must see" experiences skipped over in previous days, with a couple of unique bits of fun for a day that is all about making memories. Go all out and make the last day of your trip one of the best, making sure you return home filled with the same sense of wonder you experienced on your first day in New York City.

The Heart of the City - Explore Times Square

Just like the city it so encapsulates, Times Square goes by many names: the Crossroads of the World, The Center of the Universe, and the heart of The Great White Way. Once upon a time it went by yet another name, Longacre Square, after London's carriage district which the area mimicked. It got the designation of Times Square in 1904 after the New York Times, one of the world's most read and revered news outlets, moved its offices here. Perhaps the reason it has so many names is that summing it up in a few words is nearly impossible.

Here you will see such famous sights as the location of the annual New Year's Eve ball drop, the giant steaming Cup O' Noodles, and more digital billboards than almost any place else on earth. There are famous street performers and a constant and rotating cast of costumed characters to amuse children, as well as provide photo opportunities (**PLEASE NOTE:** Many of these street performers and characters will expect, or demand, a small donation for a family photo. We do not recommend that you take a picture without finding out the cost first). There is also a wide array of stores, including a massive, multi-story Toys R' Us that has a working Ferris wheel inside.

Travel Tip: Among the famed billboards and neon lights, one stands out and deserves a look. A new digital billboard spanning an entire city block, on Broadway from 45th to 46th street, will amaze families as they enjoy what over 24 million LED pixels looks like - displaying everything from digital art to advertising. Take a quick stop and enjoy the free show.

While gentrification and efforts to clean up the city have taken it a long way from the former red light district that Times Square once was, some small vestiges remain. There are a few adult stores littering the edges of the area, something parents should be aware of. They are located mostly near the Port Authority Bus Terminal, and the quicker you push into the heart of the area the better off you will be. This is one of the most heavily patrolled and monitored parts of the city, so don't worry excessively about safety. However, it is a very busy place filled with all sorts of people, so be very watchful and keep close, as the busy and congested streets can make it easy to get separated.

We recommend starting the day here, preferably just after rush hour (there are so many offices in and around the area, and navigating the streets during the morning commute will be tricky) and taking in the area before it gets too busy with the midday rush of tourists. Try to be the first "out of towners" here and enjoy a *relatively* quiet time taking in the sights and popping into any stores that interest you.

Address: Located at the junction of Broadway and Seventh Avenue, spanning from West 42nd to West 47th Streets.

Hours: This open area is in use 24/7. We advise getting here as early as possible to avoid crowds and make the most of your last day.

Getting Here: Nearly every Manhattan subway line converges on Times Square, with the 42nd Street/Port Authority Bus Terminal station being serviced by the 1, 2, 3, 7, A, C, E, N, Q, R, and S lines.

Website: www.timessquarenyc.org/index.aspx

Approximate Cost: No admission. Also, though there is a lot of shopping here, some shops are very expensive so pay close attention to the prices.

Approximate Time: We advise spending about a **half hour** here, which should be enough time to take it in before moving on to the rest of the day.

A Different Kind of Tour - Experience "The Ride"

Having had a chance to explore Times Square on your own, it is time to see it from a different angle and as part of a unique experience. While you may or may not retread some of the same ground you just saw on your own, now you have a chance to do so with new eyes, ears, and the benefit of a humorous, friendly guide to make sense of it all.

Billed as "Part Tour, Part Ride" this unique attraction has entertained many NYC visitors with its exciting new brand of family experience. The 75 minute interactive tour features stadium seating and a panoramic view, all in a multi-million dollar custom built vehicle that allows you to experience New York like never before. See midtown and Times Square, along with street performances, trivia, karaoke, and the fun of professional, comedic hosts.

It will be fun to see what you managed to pick out on your own, compared to what you passed over. The context and background gained from a professional guide will be interesting, and the fun and humor of the experience is tailored to families, helping keep children excited and engaged. This is a great way to get your children ready for the rest of the day, with a shot of energy that will carry you through and help you make the most of this last day.

PLEASE NOTE: This is not an inexpensive excursion. While we feel it is worth it for families who really want to see and do more, if the cost is too much, simply spend more time in the area exploring on your own.

Address: 234 W 42nd St, New York, NY 10036

Phone: (646) 289-5060

Hours: Monday - Saturday, 10 AM - 8 PM. Sunday 10 AM - 4:30 PM.

Getting Here: "The Ride" is actually located in Times Square, so just try to wind down your exploration of the area on 42nd Street, between 7th and 8th Avenues.

Website: http://experiencetheride.com/

Approximate Cost: All tickets are $74 (though there are often coupons available), you can buy online in advance of your trip to guarantee a spot. Tickets are $55 each for groups of 10 or more, and $35 each for school and camp groups. Contact groupsales@experiencetheride.com for advance reservations.

Approximate Time: The tour lasts **an hour and 15 minutes**.

A Quick Break - Lunch in Bryant Park

This park, just to the east of Times Square, was designated as public property by then New York Colonial Governor Thomas Dongan in 1686. It became the site of a retreat by American Troops during the Revolutionary War. Later, it became part of the Croton Reservoir and distributing center, a massive four acre lake, surrounded by giant, fifty-foot-high walls. This construction, completed in 1842, was one of the greatest engineering achievements of the 19th century and supplied much of New York City's water at the time. During the Civil War, Bryant Park, then called "reservoir square" was used as an encampment for Union Army troops.

At the end of the 19th century, the reservoir was demolished to coincide with the construction of new water tunnels that would take over the task of supplying New York City with water. The land was used for the construction of a new library building and park. You can still see a remnant of the reservoir at the foundation of the South Court of the New York Public Library, as well as a historical plaque located on the wall in the underground passageway that connects the Fifth Avenue and 42nd Street subway stations.

After a revival in the 1990's Bryant Park's storied history opened a new chapter as the "Town Square of Midtown." Here you'll find office workers taking lunch on weekdays, tourists taking in the ambiance, along with a host of events, performances, and assorted fun. Here you will also find the main branch of the New York Public Library. While technically within the bounds of the park itself, in practice the stunning 1911 construction forms an eastern border for the usable area of the park.

Travel Tip: Since 2002, every year there are a series of holiday shops in Bryant Park from roughly late October through early January. Modelled after the European Christkindlmarkt, these charming seasonal shops offer food and gifts, representing both independent offering and small outposts of major retailers.

Bryant Park has a lot to offer families on any given day, from the Reading Room and Le Carrousel to games like chess & backgammon or even ping pong. You should also check the calendar to see if any events coincide with your visit. The park is a magnet for upscale food trucks, as well as playing host to a number of small cafes and eateries. The surrounding blocks also offer a lot in the way of food.

Take some time to relax and stretch your legs in this beautiful midtown setting. Grab a bite as you sit and admire the library, and take part in some classic New York City people-watching as you see some of the thousands of individuals who make their way through Bryant Park on a given day.

Address: Located between 5th and 6th Avenues, spanning 40th to 42nd Streets

Phone: (212) 768-4242

Hours: Open weekdays from 7 AM - Midnight. Weekends from 7 AM - 11 PM.

Getting Here: A 4-5 minute **cab** ride from the last stop, or 5 minutes by 7 **train** from Times Square to 5th Avenue. If you are up for it, the few blocks are about a third of a mile and can be walked in about 10 minutes.

Website: www.bryantpark.org/

Approximate Cost: Free to sit in the park, food varies by location.

Approximate Time: We recommend **a half hour to an hour** here depending on if you shop as well, to keep up your pace for the day.

A True Classic - Tour the Empire State Building

One of New York City's most recognizable landmarks, the Empire State building is a 102 story skyscraper, completed in 1931. Deriving its name from New York State's nickname, "The Empire State," with a total height of 1,454 feet (including its spire) it was the world's tallest building for nearly 40 years. Currently it is the 5th tallest skyscraper in the United States (2nd in New York City, behind One World Trade Center) and 25th tallest in the world.

All this height means that it enjoys some of the most amazing views in all of New York City, with an uninterrupted, 360 degree panorama that includes the entirety of the five boroughs, New Jersey, and beyond. This is the perfect opportunity for your family to reflect on your entire trip, viewing everything you have seen from one place, and marveling at the sheer size of New York City from its most famous vantage point.

Beyond just the views, the building is a cultural icon, representing a stellar example of the Art Deco style that characterizes some of the most famous buildings in the city (Rockefeller Center being another great example of the style) and a heyday of large constructions and unbridled vision. The building has been named one of the Seven Wonders of the Modern World by the American Society of Civil Engineers, and the Empire State Building has been featured in countless works of film and television, famously climbed by King Kong in just one of a number of iconic portrayals.

Fun Fact: The Empire State Building is a lightning rod for the area of midtown Manhattan. It is struck by lightning an average of 23 times per year.

For your visit, after waiting in line (or skipping, thanks to an express ticket) you will have access to the lobby, replete with stunning Art Deco murals. The second floor houses a new exhibit dedicated to sustainability. On the 80th floor, following your impressively speedy elevator ride, you'll find the "Dare to Dream Exhibit", which takes you and your family inside the process of designing and constructing this famous landmark. One final elevator ride will take you to the 86th floor and the main observation deck to enjoy the famous views.

An interactive multimedia tour is included with every ticket, giving you a deeper understanding of the building, its place in history, and its leadership today. This handheld multimedia experience is available in English, Spanish, French, Italian, Mandarin, Portuguese, Japanese, and Korean.

While it may be considered by many as "touristy", there is good reason over 110 million people have visited the Empire State Building. There are the fascinating exhibits, which help convey the ambition and "can do" attitude of New Yorkers. Add to that the views that help bring your entire journey together into one location - and you have an unforgettable experience and an important family memory to share.

Address: 350 5th Ave, New York, NY 10118

Hours: Daily, 8 AM - 2 AM (365 days a year, regardless of weather).

Getting Here: A 5 minute **cab** ride from Bryant Park, or 5-10 minutes by train. Take the M towards Middle Village or the F towards Coney Island, getting off at 34th Street/Herald Square, then walk across town to 5th Avenue. If you are up for a walk (and want to see some things on the way) the journey of just under half a mile should take about 10-15 minutes.

Website: www.esbnyc.com/

Approximate Cost: Adults, $32. Children (6-12), $26. You can also opt for an express package, which lets you skip the lines, for a flat $55 per person. You should buy your tickets online in advance if possible.

Approximate Time: We recommend **an hour to an hour and a half**. Unless you opt for the express ticket, which promises to get you to the top in 10 minutes, wait times can be around a half hour, give or take, before you can get to the top and start touring. See their website for an estimated wait time for general admission, updated every 2 minutes.

Some High Speed Fun - Ride "The BEAST" Speedboat

PLEASE NOTE: This attraction is seasonal, and runs from May-September every year. If travelling outside of those times, you can stay longer at one of the other stops today (including the next stop at The Intrepid), or see **Appendix A** for an alternate to swap in.

The Beast is a unique, seasonal speedboat that is operated by Circle Line Sightseeing Cruises. This New York Harbor cruise company "unleashed The BEAST" in 2011, offering New York City's fastest speedboat opportunity. The boat looks like something out of a Viking myth, with a whimsical face painted on the sides of the long hull. The BEAST features 1400 horsepower engines that allow the boat to get up to a top speed of around 40 knots, approximately 45 miles per hour.

There are **safety considerations** that may limit your ability to ride "The BEAST." You cannot ride if you are pregnant, have a heart condition, back problem, or susceptibility to back injuries. **Children must be at least 40"** (3 feet, 4 inches) tall to ride, and must be able to sit in their own seat without assistance.

If your children aren't tall enough, or the high speed isn't for you, note that Circle Line *also offers other, more relaxing sightseeing tours that suit all ages and tastes, in case you still feel like taking to the water, but at your own pace.*

Head down towards New York Harbor with the family, blazing along at high speed as you once again take in the tall buildings of One World Trade Center, the World Financial Center, as well as Ellis Island and the Statue of Liberty (which you will actually get within 100 feet of). The whole family will enjoy the great views of midtown and lower Manhattan, the exciting soundtrack, and the informative and exciting crew. Children will love the speed and excitement, as you up the ante and keep your energy high for the rest of the day.

Travel Tip: Make sure to secure all your personal belongings as the ride does get bumpy. Keep cameras, wallets, and the like in pockets or bags so you don't lose them. It is best to also stow hats or sunglasses to avoid having them fly off while the boat is at full speed. Also be warned, you will most likely get a little wet, not in an uncomfortable way, but you may want to keep it in mind when you dress for the day.

While you have crossed a few bridges, and seen the bottom of Manhattan from the Staten Island Ferry, this high speed journey along the length of the island will present a unique vantage point from which to appreciate the city you have been touring. Have fun, let loose, and recognize that it really is possible to do just about anything you can imagine in New York City!

Address: Pier 83 West 42nd Street, New York, NY 10036

Phone: (212) 563-3200

Hours: Daily, 10 AM - 6 PM. Tours leave every hour, on the hour. (**NOTE**: Only Open May - September) The BEAST does not operate when raining.

Getting Here: A 20 minute **cab** ride from The Empire State Building, or about 25 minutes by public transit. Take the N, Q or R **train** towards Astoria to Times Square, followed by a 1 mile crosstown walk. The better bet is to take the **bus**, walking to 42nd Street and 5th Avenue, then taking the M42 crosstown towards the 42nd Street Pier, getting off at the last stop, directly in front of the pier.

Website: www.ridethebeast.com/

Approximate Cost: Adults, $29. Children (3-12), $23.

Approximate Time: The ride lasts about a half hour, though your stop here will take **up to an hour** when you factor in time to get on and off, safety demonstrations, and other considerations.

Board an Aircraft Carrier - Tour the Intrepid Sea, Air & Space Museum

Intrepid (CV-11) is one of 24 Essex-class aircraft carriers built during World War II. Intrepid would go on to serve in the Pacific Theater. Decommissioned following the armistice, the ship eventually went back into service, seeing action in the Vietnam War, and serving as a recovery vessel for multiple space missions. Intrepid was decommissioned for the last time in 1974, brought to New York City, and in 1982 became the setting for this unique and immersive museum.

While there are display areas and information on Pier 86, the pier at which the ship is docked, the bulk of this museum is actually aboard the massive 38,000 ton "Fighting I" aircraft carrier. This allows you and your family to stand in the footsteps of the service men that sailed her across the world. The museum highlights "history, science, and service" for a special combination of disciplines that explain our past, the mechanics of aviation and seafaring, as well as the proud traditions of the military.

On the top of the ship's open area lies the flight deck; here you and your family can see more than two dozen restored aircraft, from a variety of eras and representing a wide array of functions. You will also enjoy great views of the Hudson River, as you gaze at midtown Manhattan on the one side, and New Jersey across the way. Going below, you'll encounter the gallery deck, with authentic military locales like the combat information center (CIC) and squadron ready room. The third deck takes you inside the life of a sailor, with living quarters, a mess hall, and insight into what it was like to serve on this ship. Finally, the hangar deck features the main exhibit space, with a more traditional museum set up, and displays related to science and service.

The museum also includes several additional areas, dedicated to some of the most amazing technology in the history of air, sea and space:

- Submarine Growler, is a decommissioned guided missile submarine, the only such craft open to the public in the entire United States. Tour the sub for an up-close and immersive look at submarine life.
- British Airways Concorde, the former supersonic transport (SST) that could cross the Atlantic Ocean in a record 2 hours, 52 minutes and 59 seconds. While some parents may have had a chance to experience one of these commercial airplanes, the whole family will enjoy the up close look at the technology that made them possible.
- Space Shuttle Pavilion, the new crown jewel of the Intrepid Museum, made possible after the space shuttle Enterprise was awarded to the museum by NASA in

2011. This prototype paved the way for great advances in the US space program, and the exhibit includes original artifacts, photographs, audio, and films that offer an extensive look at both the science and history of the space shuttle era.

PLEASE NOTE: The submarine *Growler* is FREE to tour with regular Museum admission. The Concorde is available to view for free, but to explore the inside you must be part of a guided tour group; access to the Space Shuttle Pavilion requires an additional ticket.

Part of the beauty of the Intrepid Air, Sea & Space Museum is the variety it offers. Children (and adults) can delight in the exhibits on multiple levels, whether their interests lie in the history, the science, or the human element. For those with children of varying ages and/or interests, this is a fantastic place to visit as everyone can find something on their level.

Address: Pier 86 W 46th St and 12th Ave, New York, NY 10036

Phone: (212) 245-0072

Hours: Weekdays, 10 AM - 5 PM. Weekends/Holidays, 10 AM - 6 PM. Please Note: in the Fall/Winter (November-April) the Museum closes at 5 PM every day.

Getting Here: About 5 minutes by **cab** from The Beast if you are really tired. Your best bet is to **walk**, the four blocks (about a fifth of a mile) should only take a few minutes.

Website: www.intrepidmuseum.org/

Approximate Cost: General Admission is $24 for Adults, $19 for Youths (7-17) and $12 for Children (3-6). Specialty tours, the space shuttle pavilion, and other features cost extra. You can book online and see prices for the full range of activities.

Approximate Time: We recommend about **1 1/2 - 2 hours** to take it all in, though this is your last stop so you can adjust depending on how much time you have left in your schedule. Just remember to factor in travel time to your final destination, and if you want to get in any last minute shopping or picture taking.

Wrap Up and Head Home - Last Minute Shopping and Considerations

While everyone's itinerary, departure time, and other nitty-gritty details will vary - it is important to build in some flex time. It may be a last minute trip to pick up orders for gifts you might have placed, or to buy the souvenirs you weren't sure about and thought you might go back for. It may be a quick meal to fill you up for the trip, or a shopping spree for last minute keepsakes and gifts to bring home.

Besides the fact that you need to allow some time as a contingency against the unexpected, it is always nice to have a little padding at the end of a long trip in case anyone feels they may have missed something. Did you never get around to trying that ice cream shop that the kids have been begging you to go to? Never found something for a cousin's upcoming birthday? Fill in your last minute needs *and* last minute wants. Check in with the kids, see what is on everyone's list and accomplish as much as you can. You can sleep when you get home!

Logistics - Day 7

Suggested Order of Stops:
1. Times Square
2. "The Ride"
3. Lunch in Bryant Park
4. Empire State Building
5. "The Beast" Speedboat Ride
6. Intrepid Sea, Air & Space Museum

Things to Bring/Note:
- Comfortable shoes for a day with a bit of walking.
- Don't forget to take extra pictures of your last day, and fill in any gaps you might have missed in terms of city photos, pictures of the kids, or group shots.
- As with all the Manhattan days, a MetroCard will be a good idea considering the ease of getting around the island by subway.
- Note that if you choose to ride **The Beast**, you will likely get a little wet, and you will need to be able to secure valuables, hats, and sunglasses for a quick and bumpy ride. Plan accordingly when you dress for the day, and bring along a bag to stash things in while on the boat.
- Pack layers in an easily accessible place, in an outside pocket or the top of the clothes in your suitcase, so you can grab them before your flight (if flying home).
- Be sure to double check room to not leave anything behind.
- Double check outlets to make sure you haven't left chargers plugged in and forgotten.
- Pack reading material, small games, and other entertainment to keep children happy during the return trip.
- Fully charge devices for the flight/drive/ride back.
- Be sure to download music, movies, eBooks and other digital materials before leaving.

Part V of the accompanying children's stories goes with today's itinerary. We recommend reading the story the night before, or morning of today's journey. After that, enjoy the epilogue, and round out the children's story along with your vacation.

Our Hope for You

Throughout this book we have endeavored to provide the best in background information, quality activities and excursions, as well as connections to quality providers within New York City.

From great museums to famous landmarks, glimpses of the historical past to cultural experiences in the present - we hope we have been able to provide a well-rounded look at a city with so much to offer families.

While 7 days is barely enough time to scratch the surface on a visit to New York City, what we have put together has hopefully been able to give you and your children an overview of different areas, as well as a background on the city's amazing story - we hope this has been a nice sampling of what New York has to offer.

As a family vacation is as much about the company as it is the destination; we hope that seeing these sights and experiencing these journeys together as a family will provide you with incredible opportunities for bonding, for growth, and for getting to know each other better as you get to know this amazing place.

Now may be the time to venture home, but it should not be an end to the experience. We hope you took lots of pictures, which you will all enjoy sharing with one another, as well as friends and extended family. It is a great way to relive vacation memories and hold on to the experiences for years to come. We also recommend following up your trip with family discussions. Talk about the things you said and did while away. Keep an eye on the news and share about developments that may interest your children, as they have a new investment in a people and place they may not have fully understood before.

Whether it was standing amid the bright lights, marveling together at a beautiful view, loving the same work of art, or learning something none of you had heard before - hold dear the feelings that made the trip special and do your best to relive them after your return. That same closeness, that same emotion can be yours at home, as you and your children have experienced something together that no one can ever take away.

Children's Story: Time Travelling Siblings in NYC

To help augment the experience of children travelling to New York City and families using this book as a guide, we have included this fun tale of adventure and intrigue as three young children travel through time on their family trip to New York.

A work of historical fiction, meant to be enjoyed by children, young adults, and the family as a whole - this story will help lend context and an element of excitement to your trip. Read it before you go to build up anticipation, or on evenings during the trip as a bedtime story to tease the next day's activities or reflect on what you just saw.

Keeping children engaged, and offering something for every member of the family on their own level, is an important part of our mission. This fun and educational "book within a book" is aimed to help accomplish that.

The story is broken into six parts (five stories, with an epilogue), and takes place at locations actually included in the main itinerary. While it can be read all in one shot, we have broken it up to allow the events of the story to unfold alongside your vacation. At various points throughout the 7 day trip we have included references to come here, labeled Story Part I, Part II, etc. We encourage you to read it as a serial piece in this manner, letting the events of the main characters fuel your own children's senses of wonder, imagination, and excitement as they explore New York City themselves.

We hope you and your children enjoy this opportunity to let history "come alive" and encourage you to learn as you go. You may also want to allow children to read it themselves, and serve as "teachers" for the rest of the family as you go on your trip. The possibilities for fun are endless. Enjoy!

Part I

The bright summer sun was shining overhead on a hot July day, illuminating the lush green spaces of Central Park that surrounded Sophia. A clever and thoughtful 12 year old, Sophia was walking quickly down one of the many paved walkways in the center of the park, making sure not to lose sight of her brother Avery.

Despite his good intentions and big heart, 9 year old Avery has a reputation for mischief in the family. He never really *causes* any trouble, but his wanderings sometimes get the better of him. Sophia was also wary because their 4 year old sister Vera, the real firecracker of the family, was holding her brother tight as they traversed the open areas of Central Park.

The family vacation to New York City was off to a great start, after an exciting morning at the Museum of Natural History. With a world of dinosaurs running around in their minds, the trio was excited to see what else the city had to offer.

Sophia had one eye on their parents and older siblings, who had pressed on ahead towards the water, and her other on the playful duo she knew she *really* needed to pay attention to. As the rest of the family eyed the paddleboats circulating the pond area, Sophia saw her younger siblings starting to wander.

Adorable Vera, her hair in pigtails and wearing a smile brighter than all the lights in Times Square, had taken to skipping along, humming a song that only she knew. Chuckling to herself about Vera's ability to find fun anywhere, Sophia temporarily lost sight of her brother.

Avery, with his wide eyes and curious streak, had spotted something that interested him. Standing tall atop a wooden box, was a man painted in bright silver, performing the moves of a human robot. The man's metallic finish, from the peak of his sequined top hat to the bright finish of his shoes, caught the midday sun and made his accentuated movements even more fun to watch. With small whirs and hisses, like gears grinding and valves letting off steam, he pumped his arms and did a really good job of pretending to be a mechanical man.

Avery was impressed with this automated performer. The robot man paused, slowly turned his head in a perfect sideways motion, and clicked his arm to an upright position. As the "robot" tipped his hat to the young boy, Avery reached into his pocket for one of the shiny quarters he always carried on family trips.

Sophia caught sight of this out of the corner of her eye, just as she had collected a skipping Vera from the other side of the path.

"Avery!" she exclaimed, reminding her brother to pay attention to the family, and not just the performers in the park.

Sophia, clutching Vera tight, rushed over to her brother just as he dropped a quarter into the robot man's hat.

Just then, something happened.

The three siblings stood at the feet of the mechanical performer, who smiled at them and winked as he raised the hat back towards his head. All three siblings saw a great flash of light, like the sun had caught his silver finish and blinded them all for just a second.

They heard a whooshing sound, like the one made as the man had "adjusted" his robot arms, but much louder. Had they had a second to think about it, they might have realized that the flash of light couldn't have possibly come from the street performer either - but it all happened so fast. In a blaze of light and a roar of sound, the children were quickly stunned, almost as much as they would be by what came next.

"What was that?" Vera asked, clearly confused, and rubbing eyes that smarted from the flash of light.

"You saw it too?" Avery added, thinking he had been the only one.

Dependable Sophia, not one to let her parents down, was also confused; though right now she had bigger things to worry about. She grabbed her siblings by their hands, and turned towards the water to find their family. There was just one problem.

When they all looked towards the water, their parents weren't there. Neither were their older siblings. In fact, there was no one to be seen at all.

More than a little concerned, Sophia quickly spun around to where the robot man had been standing, only to find that he too was gone. None of the people who had surrounded them just a moment before were there anymore.

"Where did everyone go?" asked Avery, putting words to what they were all thinking.

Just then, they did hear *something*.

"Striiiiiiiiiiiiike!" a voice called out, echoing over the open area of the park.

"Is that a baseball game? Avery asked.

Avery's question was met with a definitive answer, in the form of the loudest clanging sound the three had every head. A loud chorus of smashing, cracking, and banging sounds rang out for a few brief seconds, throwing the trio off balance.

As Avery and Sophia stood still, holding their ears at the tremendous noise, Vera ran forward.

"Hooooooooooold!" called the voice once again, giving brief pause to the clanging.

Never one to shy away from anything, an excited Vera actually ran *towards* the sound, up and over a nearby hill. As her older siblings scrambled to catch up, Vera began jumping up and down and pointing. As the three siblings stood at the top of the hill, looking downward, they saw the source of the noise.

"Striiiiiiiiiiiiiike!" called out the man, clutching a stack of papers to his dusty coveralls.

Just as the man finished his cry, a long line of men standing in front of him lowered their pickaxes against the large rocks that lay before them. The sound of metal on stone rang loud through the field again, like nothing the children had ever heard before.

"Wow!" Vera exclaimed, echoing the sentiment they all shared.

It was clever Sophia that realized there was something wrong with this picture. "Why are they breaking rocks by hand? Shouldn't they use a machine for that?"

"You're right," Avery added. "When they built the new park at our school, they used a backhoe that just hauled them all out at once."

The siblings looked at each other quizzically, wondering what kind of operation was going on in the park, and where their parents had gone.

Just then, their pondering was interrupted by another loud sound.

"Neiiiiigh!" came a loud braying, from a horse stopping hard in its tracks, right behind the children. The horse kicked up its front legs, nearly tossing the well-dressed man atop it.

"Pardon me young ones" the man said, gathering the reins in his gloved hands and starting off slower, to walk his horse around the children.

"Whoa, that was a close one" said Avery, not keen on being caught under a horse's foot. "Imagine being run over by a police horse!"

"But that wasn't a police horse," Sophia pointed out.

"Sure it was, didn't you see his dark shirt, and the black boots?" Avery asked, reciting details he had noticed upon spotting his first mounted officer earlier in the day.

"But he didn't have a badge, or a helmet!" Sophia pointed out.

The children all turned to see that Sophia was right. In fact, the man was wearing clothes like they had never seen before. His dark shirt fit loosely, and was tucked into pants that seemed to balloon out at his thighs. As he galloped off down the path it was the first time the children had noticed that the usual asphalt was missing, replaced by a muddy track that was out of character for Central Park.

Just as they lost sight of the man, they heard the clopping of more hooves coming up behind them. Lots more. Soon more horses, with ordinary men and women atop them, began to filter past. Then came the carriages. The black boxes with large wooden wheels and open windows were like something out of a movie. Inside were men and women, dressed like they were heading out for a night on the town. Women in beautiful dresses, ribbed tops that rose to their necks, and bustles that seemed to fill the entire carriage with lacy fabric. The men wore coats with shiny gold buttons, tall hats, and funny, loose ties flapping about their necks.

The children had never seen a real life carriage before, nor had they seen so many people on horses in one place. Come to think of it, the oddest part was how well dressed everyone seemed to be, like they had been diverted from a charity event to quickly hop on a horse in the park.

All the horses and horse drawn vehicles seemed to he headed in the same direction, around a bend just up ahead. The children decided to follow, curious as to what was developing. They were sure that with something this exciting, their parents must have caught an interest as well, and they could find them at wherever everyone was heading.

The three siblings excitedly rounded the bend, coming to an open area filled with simple chairs and a small stage.

The people began filing out of their carriages, dismounting their horses and arranging themselves around the stage. Women with long white gloves and delicate parasols greeted each other and shared warm hugs under the hot sun. Men gathered in smaller circles, telling jokes and laughing loudly as they tied their horses to nearby posts.

Over time, from the other direction, more people started to appear over the hill at the far end of the clearing. These columns of people advanced more slowly, clearly struggling to keep up with the midday heat. They wore clothes that were far simpler than the horse and carriage crowd, but still far more elaborate than what the siblings were used to - at least for a day in the park. There wasn't a T-shirt or pair of shorts to be seen.

This second group of people made their way around the path to the same green area the horses and their riders occupied. As both groups surrounded the stage, a third group came off from yet another direction. These men all carried instruments, and made their way up onto the small wooden platform. As they sat down, a hush fell over the previously boisterous crowd amassed around it. Those who had rode in and those who had walked sat side by side, eagerly awaiting what was to come.

"Oh cool, a concert!" Avery exclaimed, excited that anything really could happen in New York City, at any given time.

The music began. It was classical, slow and melodic, though it was difficult to make out over the vast distance of the field. The lack of speakers, microphones, or anything else to amplify the sound wasn't lost on the children.

"It's beautiful," Sophia added, as young Vera began dancing in place to the music.

Just then, an odd scene got even odder.

"Striiiiiiiiiiiiiike!" came the now familiar call, followed by the familiar clanging.

The three children jumped in place, alarmed at the sound. The clanging and the music continued at the same time, though they seemed to be the only ones bothered by it. To one side, men in coveralls broke rocks. To the other, men in jackets strummed violins and cellos. It was confusing and beautiful at the same time - like nothing they had expected.

The children looked at each other, then turned to see a man coming up behind them.

"Beautiful concert, isn't it kids?" the man asked.

"It sure is" replied Sophia. She knew she shouldn't talk to strangers, but felt it impolite to not respond before motioning to her siblings to step away.

Also knowing better than to talk to a man he didn't know, but too curious to help himself, Avery just had to ask: "What are you doing there?" Avery inquired, looking at the paper and pencil in the man's hand.

"Taking a count on attendance in the new park for the New York Times. Yessir, looks like we're going to top two and a half million for the year of 1860!"

"1860!?!?" The trio exclaimed, finally realizing they were in for more than they bargained for.

Part II

It was hard to say whether it was the heat of the sun, the fact that they hadn't eaten in hours, or the recent revelation that they were in the year 1860 that had the three siblings so thrown off balance.

Come to think of it, chances are it was that last one.

Sophia, Avery, and Vera stood in a field trying to make sense of just what was going on right now.

"Where are mommy and daddy?" Vera asked, noting her primary concern.

"I don't know Vera, I think first we need to figure out where we are." Sophia pointed out.

"Yeah," Avery added, "and we need to get away from this guy who thinks its 1860!"

"I'm not sure he's wrong," Sophia offered. "Think about what we saw in that park. There were none of the buildings, or the paved roads that had been there when we entered. The clothes everyone had on seemed like they were out of the 19th century, and the park wasn't even finished!"

"You're right," said Avery. "Those guys breaking rocks looked like they were clearing out the area. Mom and Dad had told us that Central Park only opened in 1857, and that they were still working on it for years!"

"Mommy and Daddy!" Vera repeated, echoing her earlier insistence.

"You're right Vera. If we really did travel back in time, somehow, to the 1800's, then we need to figure out how to get back. We need to find our family!"

The three looked at each other intently, nodding in silent agreement. Then Avery spoke up:

"There is just one more problem," Avery pointed out. "Where are we *now*?"

The three siblings looked around, pondering Avery's question. They were in an open green space, just steps away from a dense forested area. Trees of all types obscured the horizon, but the lack of tall buildings was noticeable despite the overgrowth. Somewhere in the distance, they could hear the surging waters of what must have been a river. Birds sang in the treetops and gone were the sounds of music, rock breaking, horses or really, of anything at all.

A quick survey of the area revealed that the newspaper man was gone, as well as anyone else they had seen since their time travelling adventure had begun. They were just three kids, alone in a forest, apparently in the 1800's.

"I don't think this is Central Park anymore" Avery said. "Not even 1860 Central Park."

As his sisters nodded their heads in agreement, suddenly the trio heard a sound up ahead.

At first it was the faint snapping of twigs underfoot, though it got louder over the coming minute.

"Who's there?" Vera asked, the youngest but also boldest of the siblings.

As if to answer her question, a man began to appear at the edge of the forest. He was not particularly tall, but very slender. Atop his wiry frame was a youthful face, with a very strong beard that filled out his otherwise sunken features. His slight frame was further hidden by a large tweed jacket that buttoned almost up to his neck.

He walked with purpose, an excited spring in his step as he gingerly edged around the many plants. At first, Avery thought the man might have been playing one of his favorite games from when he was Vera's age - "the floor is lava." After a few more seconds it was obvious that his main concern was for all the plants, as the man carefully avoided stepping on a single living thing.

"I saiiiiiiid, who are you?" Vera repeated, with a genuine earnestness and curiosity in her voice.

The man stopped, turned, and looked over the three children. He clearly hadn't been ignoring them, but rather was completely oblivious to their presence. The look on his face said he wasn't annoyed or confused to now learn he wasn't alone, but he seemed torn by the idea that he had to abandon his task of looking over the plants around him.

"Ah, pardon me young ones. Allow me to introduce myself; my name is Nathaniel Lord Britton. Who may I ask are you, such young children with such peculiar clothing?"

Ignoring the comment about their clothes, thinking *he* should be the one talking, Avery was the first to respond.

"My name is Avery, and these are my sisters, Sophia and Vera."

"Very pleased to make your acquaintance Avery, Sophia, and Vera" Nathaniel responded, quickly turning back to look at the plants.

"Yes, well excuse me Mr. Britton, but we are lost and trying to find out where we are, and…" Sophia began, interrupted before she could say "when."

"Please, call me Nathaniel!" the main responded. A visible spark in his eyes had finally pulled his attention from the surrounding plants. They had clearly gotten him excited enough to deserve his full attention. "And where you are is not really anywhere, yet, but very soon it will be the finest and most exciting place in all of New York City!"

"Niketown!?" Avery guessed, referring to his own personal idea of excitement.

"Well, no...And I can't say I'm certain what that means," Nathaniel responded. "You children are standing on the future site of the New York City Botanical Garden, my life's work and the most exciting development in the history of our growing city."

"Wait, so we're in The Bronx right now?" Sophia asked, remembering the location from the plan for the family's vacation.

"Indeed you are," Nathaniel continued. "All of this land used to belong to a family by the name of Lorillard, who used it for farming and shipping, but through the hard work of my wife and I the city has taken it on for the purpose of building a glorious garden space!"

"So you started...err...are *starting* the New York Botanical garden yourself?" Avery asked.

"Well, not myself. With the help of some wonderful men and women," a now visibly excited Nathaniel continued. "The idea came to my darling wife Elizabeth and me during our honeymoon in England. We visited Kew Gardens, the Royal Botanic Gardens of London and were inspired by their majestic presentation, and the research being done there. With New York City quickly becoming a place the world looks to for insight and knowledge, we believe this is the perfect place for an equally beautiful and forward thinking garden for Americans to get excited about."

"So you and your wife are making all this possible?" Sophia asked, finding Nathaniel's excitement contagious.

"Elizabeth and I, along with many of New York City's finest citizens. Mr. Andrew Carnegie, J. Pierpont Morgan, and Cornelius Vanderbilt II have all been instrumental in the project, as in so many other New York City advancements."

"I have heard of those names," Sophia added.

"I am quite sure you did, everyone must have heard of them! It is truly a golden age for the city right now, with the richest and most influential citizens contributing so much to grow culture and knowledge for all New Yorkers. It is truly a dream for a young man from Staten Island such as myself to sit across from them and create something that will benefit all its citizens!"

"But why a garden?" Avery asked. "Why not something fun, like a basketball court...or the world's largest candy store!"

Sophia laughed to herself at Avery's famous love of sweets and one-track mind. Vera giggled aloud, amused by both her siblings and their familiar antics.

"Ha! I understand what you mean young man, but what makes you think we aren't in a candy store right now?" Nathaniel responded.

The three siblings looked at each other quizzically, unsure what their new friend meant.

"Follow me," Nathaniel said, as he led the children towards a nearby tree.

Sophia, Avery, and Vera watched as Nathaniel stopped at the tree. He reached into his pocket and produced a small knife with one hand, as he reached up to the branches with another. He pulled a small, ripe apple from the tree and lowered it to his chest, polishing it against his rough coat. He opened the knife and carefully cut small wedges, which he handed to the children.

An eager Avery, eyes wide at the proposition of a treat, looked to his older sister for approval. Vera did as well. As the older sister nodded to say "okay", the three bit into their apple slices and marveled at the delicious taste that filled their mouth.

"Do you see what I mean?" Nathaniel asked. "Nature is the original candy store. The apples and berries of this forest are the sweet treats that men and women have enjoyed since the beginning of time."

The children watched in amusement as Nathaniel walked up to another tree, snapping off a tiny branch. He ran his knife down the length of the stick several times, stripping off the bark. He approached the children and held it up to young Vera.

"Tell me what you smell young lady" he said.

"Root beer!" Vera said, clapping her hands in amusement over the exciting trick.

Avery and Sophia gave a big whiff themselves, finding themselves similarly amazed.

"How did you do that?" Sophia asked.

"I did nothing my young friend. This is a native birch tree, and the youngest branches are full of the sweet sap that is brewed to flavor delicious sodas."

"That is *so* cool!" Avery exclaimed.

"Indeed," said Nathaniel. "When I was around your age, I already knew the names of almost all the plants that grew around my parent's home. The chance to educate children and other New Yorkers is part of the reason Elizabeth and I wanted to start a great public garden in the city. We also hope to give New Yorkers a space to be proud of, to help propel New York City to the forefront of culture and knowledge. Finally, we hope to promote science, and provide a space for research that will advance our shared knowledge of plant life."

"To create more, and even better sodas!" Avery exclaimed, with a thought that had occurred to no one else.

The group fell silent for just a second, until Sophia spoke up to renew an old concern.

"Thank you for teaching us so much about plants and the Botanical Garden, but can we ask you one more thing?"

"But of course my friends!" Nathaniel responded. "What would you like to know about? My lectures at Columbia University? Or perhaps my research on the native flora of the Caribbean?"

"Actually," Sophia continued, "this has nothing to do with plants. We seem to be separated from our parents and we don't know where to find them. Do you think you might be able to help? You see…"

Nathaniel perked up, once again excited and once again cutting off Sophia before she could mention anything about being stuck in the wrong century.

"I think I may just be able to help you!" Nathaniel started. "If you could just follow me to the old mill I think I might have an idea on where to find them!"

As Nathaniel began to scurry ahead, the three siblings followed. Although they had no idea how he planned on helping them, especially without really knowing the entirety of their story, it was still a better bet than standing alone in the woods.

Avery, Sophia, and Vera arrived at the door to a large stone building on the edge of the river they had heard before. A great wooden wheel turned with the rushing water. Nathaniel pressed on ahead, opening the door and ushering the children inside. The grateful children followed him in, waiting to see what would come next…

Part III

As the three children stepped through the door, they found themselves not inside an old water mill as they had expected, but rather in a vast corn field that felt a world away from the forest they had just been in.

"Ok, this is getting even weirder" Avery said, turning to his sisters for agreement.

"What just happened?" Sophia added, amazed at the seamless transition that seemed to walk them through time and space from The Bronx to…who knows where…in a split second.

"Where is Nathaniel?" Vera added, as the three looked around to notice that their previous companion was noticeably absent from their new surroundings.

"First we're standing in Central Park with our family, then we're in the same place but 150 years in the past. Then, suddenly we're miles away in The Bronx!" Sophia said, thinking out loud to try and make sense of the situation.

"And still in the past" Avery pointed out. "We were supposed to go to the Botanical Garden with our family. It *has* been built, so we're back sometime before that."

"We *were* back sometime before that. Who knows where we are now," Sophia continued. "It seems like we just randomly turn around, or go through a door, or see a light, and bam! All of a sudden we've moved someplace else in the history of New York City."

"Like the museum!" Vera chimed in.

The siblings thought about it and decided it was a lot like a museum. In a few steps they could be in a different time and place, from one room to the next, except instead of looking at history behind some glass, they were standing in the middle of it.

Also, in a museum there is always a map. They had no idea where they were now.

The three siblings looked around, trying to make some sense of their surroundings. They hoped they might be able to orient themselves and figure out where they might be.

They saw vast fields of corn stretched out before them, with small wooden structures like shacks, or sheds, interspersed between them. To the other side of them was a great hill, and as they looked out over the top of it, they could see faint clouds of black smoke rising into the summer sky.

Then came a very rude awakening.

Like a roar of thunder, the clopping of hooves exploded over the hill. This was nothing like the gentle plodding of horses they had heard calmly walking through Central Park. This was a veritable explosion of sound, as horses came racing towards them at an incredible speed.

It all happened so quickly they could barely collect themselves. Vera clutched her big sister tightly and Avery stood in front of them, instinctively looking to shield his sisters. They braced themselves for what was coming.

As the horses moved to surround them, the siblings had no idea what to expect. The beasts finally slowed enough for the trio to catch a glimpse of their riders, tri-corner hats and red coats standing out brightly against the muted colors of the corn fields.

Wait a minute, the siblings thought. *Red coats*?

"Surrender your arms and kneel before the authority of King George, you colonial vagabonds!" came the call from one of the mounted men, now obviously identifiable as soldiers.

"Oh no!" Avery exclaimed, dropping to his knees and trying to find a way to lay his arms on the ground, misunderstanding what the phrase "surrender your arms" meant.

The soldiers looked on at the young boy flailing his arms about, as his sisters quietly knelt beside him, unsure what to make of the scene.

One soldier dismounted his horse, a long sword at the side of his sweeping red coat. A thick British accent accompanied his words. "It seems the colonial rebels will spare no new form of trickery, however ridiculous!" The man declared, "Sending children, in odd clothing, to spy on our operations in New York!"

The commander motioned to his cohorts to round up the three siblings, who were loaded into a cart that had just arrived at the scene. The men remounted their horses and led the cart up over the nearby hill.

"Red coats, and 'colonial trickery'!?" Sophia whispered to her brother, "I think we've just been captured by British soldiers during the Revolutionary War!"

"I think you're right," he whispered back. "But the real problem is, why does everyone keep making fun of my clothes? I love this shirt!" He added, looking down at his best soccer jersey.

Vera giggled at that comment, undeterred by the confusing situation they had landed themselves in this time.

As the cart made its way over the hill, the three siblings could make out a large and sprawling camp. There were tents as far as the eye could see. There were long, narrow ones that had men filtering in and out at a rapid pace. In between the tents were carts laden with food, barrels of water, and piles of guns and ammunition. Small campfires dotted the landscape, with men standing over them cooking food. Guards patrolled at regular intervals, and Union Jack flags flew overhead. Recognizing the symbol of Great Britain from the children's own trip to London, the trio's worst fear was confirmed: they were now prisoners of the British army.

The cart started to slow in front of the largest tent in the entire camp. The children's captors once again dismounted, surrounded the children, and in typical, well-mannered British style, helped them down off the cart. Then they were led into the tent.

Inside the tent were about a dozen men in red coats, all huddled around a large wooden table that was covered in a map. On top of the map were small figurines of soldiers, cannons, horses, and buildings. The men seemed to be moving the figures around, predicting movements and planning a large attack.

More than being frightened by these new developments, the three siblings were intensely curious. As they looked around and took in the scene a little further, the man who had first addressed the children spoke up.

"General, these colonial spies were spotted just outside of our camp. I believe that they were making their way to the Cobble Hill Fort, in order to survey our headquarters and report back on our numbers to the other rebels."

"Thank you commander, you and your men are dismissed," the general said.

He looked the children up and down for what seemed like an hour, seemingly trying to make sense of who they were. He seemed as confused as the children themselves that they had found their way to Brooklyn on the eve of an attack. Then he addressed the children directly.

"Ever since the sending of that so called 'Declaration of Independence' a month ago, you colonials have grown quite bold. Your new commander, General Washington, may think that he proved something in Boston this past March, and that a silly piece of paper meant something this July, but I assure you that by September we will have crushed this rebellion and made all of you regret ever crossing the British Crown."

"Excuse me sir, but I think this is all just a very big misunderstanding!" Sophia exclaimed. "You see, what happened was…"

Before she could finish, the British General cut her off.

"No misunderstanding my young lady. I never would have thought that Washington would stoop so low as to send children to spy for him, but it seems I underestimated his treachery."

"But we don't work for George Washington Mr. General Sir," Avery added, a little befuddled as to how he should best address the man standing before him.

"But you are on a first name basis with him?" asked another soldier.

"Well, um, no. You see…" Avery mumbled.

"Then what, pray tell, are you doing here young man? The general asked.

Avery stood to explain, when several of the quarters he carried in his pocket fell out. They clanged against each other as they hit the ground, causing the closest soldiers to jump.

The nearest soldier rushed to pick up the quarters and deliver them to his commander. As the general eyed the currency, his face twisted to an expression of genuine anger.

"And what is *this*!? Liberty? The United States of America? A quarter dollar with an image of none other than the traitor Washington himself!" The general practically yelled. "This is treasonous behavior. It seems that not only are you spies, but handsomely paid for your villainy."

"But that simply isn't true!" Sophia pleaded.

"What's villainy?" Vera asked, tugging at her sister's shirt.

"I have heard enough from you rascals! Tomorrow, when we march through the Heights of Guan you colonials will feel the full might of the British army. Soon after, you spies will be returned to England to stand trial for your offenses," the general said, a smug look on his face as he tried to scare the children.

Vera looked right back at him, refusing to be bullied by anyone.

Just then, another soldier ran into the tent, out of breath and sweating. He ran to the general's side and whispered something into his ear. The children looked on, intently.

"It seems your ill-mannered colonial friends have even more trickery afoot," the general stated, as he gathered his things to leave. "Come men, there is a situation to be dealt with. When I return, we shall deal with the young spies."

With that the general and all but two men left the tent. These two stood near the children, their backs to them, standing guard and keeping the children in place.

The trio stood in the corner of the tent, surrounded, as prisoners of the British Empire. They wondered how they were going to get out of this one. Travelling through time, separated from their parents was one thing, but now that they were literally trapped, it felt as if all might be lost.

"What are we going to do? We may not know how this time travelling works, but I think it's probably not a good idea to get sent to a British prison," Sophia said earnestly.

"You're right," Avery added, stroking his chin as if he had a goatee. "Getting out of this situation is going to take real planning. A plan so precise, so clever, that they will never see it coming…"

As Avery amused himself with putting on his best "contemplation face" and Sophia concentrated (without the funny faces) it was Vera who solved their problem.

Turning around to see the end of a rope that tied the canvas top of the tent to its poles, Vera simply tugged as hard as she could. Within seconds, the long rope began racing towards the ceiling, free of its counterbalance. Before the soldiers could react, the canvas ceiling of the tent began falling down all around them.

The children reacted quickly. After Avery snatched his quarters from the nearby table, the three siblings picked up the now loose corner of the tent and ran out.

The children could hear the guards inside yelling, now covered in the fabric of the tent that had come down around them, as soldiers from the surrounding area ran to see what the commotion was. The children didn't waste any time getting away, making a dash towards the edge of the camp.

They had no time to catch their breath.

"That *was* a clever plan!" Avery exclaimed, panting as he ran. "Nice work Vera"

Vera beamed at her big brother's compliment, as Sophia smiled too. A crowd of soldiers stood between them and the freedom of the fields beyond the camp. Not afraid of anything, the three siblings dove head first into the crowd and on towards freedom…

Part IV

Eager to escape their British captors, Avery, Sophia, and Vera had run headlong into a crowd of red coats. Taking advantage of their smaller size, they dodged between knees and waists, pushing quickly through to the other side of the crowd.

They expected to see another cornfield, or Cobble Hill, but what they found was a very different scene. There was a tall stone building in front of them, surrounded by a large mass of people. None of the people wore the red coats of British troops, and no one was acting like they were in the middle of a war.

"I think it happened again" Avery offered, panting to catch his breath from the last adventure.

Sophia, who was winded herself, nodded as she put her hands to her knees and turned her head.

"Look at the crowd, it's not the soldiers we escaped from. I think while we were running through the soldiers, we ended up somewhere else again."

Sophia, Avery, and Vera turned to survey their new surroundings. The area they were in now was certainly more established than the field they had come from, or the forest before that, but still a very far cry from the modern New York City they had started in.

"Look at that building!" Avery exclaimed. "That looks familiar."

Sophia and Vera turned to where Avery was pointing, looking past a huge crowd of people to a grand white building. The row houses and simpler wooden structures lining the open area they stood in paled in comparison to this impressive sight. With a tall steeple and massive trapezoidal roof, the front of the building was adorned with impressive columns and a great balcony.

"That's Federal Hall!" Sophia said, delighted at her own recognition. "Only not modern day Federal Hall, I recognize it from my history class!"

As the children continued to survey the scene, they noticed colorful ribbons adorning the balcony of the hall, as well as the nearby buildings. People in the crowd waved flags and fans. It was an animated group, and the children could sense the excitement in the air. This was a festive occasion, a welcome change of pace from the hostility of their last adventure.

Suddenly, a hush fell over the mass of people.

The doors of the great hall opened and people began filing out. The three siblings edged closer to get a better view.

There were a number of men in white, powdered wigs. They wore short pants with high socks, and tight fitting waistcoats that forced them to stand tall. A couple of them wore military uniforms, but not of the olive drab the children would have expected. These soldiers wore bright blue coats with gold trim, extending into long tails that were very formal. They wore swords at their sides and medals on their chest. Next came a man in the black robes of a judge.

With the end of the long procession came one final man. His reddish brown coat hugged a frilled shirt and made him look very distinguished. He wore a sword like the military men but dressed more like the ordinary men on the stage. As he made his way to the end of the balcony, the crowd erupted in a roar of cheers, whistles, claps, and overwhelming exuberance.

It was George Washington.

"No way!" Avery cried.

"Yay" Vera added.

"I can't believe it!" Sophia proclaimed, her jaw dropping.

The crowd seemed to be made up of thousands of people, all overjoyed at the sight of this great American. The man in the judge's robes was next to speak.

"Your attention please!" The man began. "I, Robert Livingston, Chancellor of New York shall now administer the oath of office, as established by resolution of Congress, to the first President Elect of the United States of America, George Washington."

Another round of cheers erupted from the crowd.

"So are we in Washington D.C. now?" Avery asked.

"No, we are on Wall Street. New York City was the first capital of the United States, the first Congress met here, and George Washington's first inauguration was here." Sophia explained, proud of what she had learned in school.

George Washington stepped up to the front of the balcony, laying his hand on the Bible placed before him.

Then Robert Livingston began, and George Washington repeated after him, the oath of office:

I do solemnly swear that I will faithfully execute the Office of President of the United States, and will to the best of my ability, preserve, protect, and defend the Constitution of the United States.

Afterwards there was a brief pause, followed by George Washington adding the words "So help me God."

This drew quizzical looks from a couple of the men on the stage, as if it had not been intended as part of the process.

Then, with all the enthusiasm of a proud parent, Robert Livingston declared, "ladies and gentlemen, I present to you the first President of the United States, Mr. George Washington!"

The sound that came next was almost deafening. Cheers erupted from the crowd, and a volley of 13 shots was fired into the air.

"This is a great day for us all, and a great day for the United States of America!" declared Mr. Livingston. "The president will now deliver his inaugural address to a joint session of the Congress. Afterwards, he will hear divine service at St. Paul's Chapel, in accordance with Congressional resolution. I wish you all a good day, and a better tomorrow for our great, new nation!"

More cheers came from the crowd

"Long live George Washington!" Livingston shouted.

The new president and the other men filed back inside the building, and the crowd began to disperse.

"This is so cool!" Avery announced. "I can't believe we got to see George Washington!"

"I know," said Sophia. "Plus, we have an idea of where we are now, and more importantly, what time period we are in. George Washington was sworn in on April 30th, 1789. So we're not exactly getting closer to our own time."

"Or mommy and daddy" Vera added, reminding everyone of their real mission.

"So where do we go from here?" Avery asked.

"That is a very good question," Sophia began. "The way I see it, we need to…"

Sophia's musings were interrupted as Vera started off in the other direction.

"Wait! Where are you going?" Avery asked, as he began to chase after his sister.

Without any warning, as if following something that only she knew, Vera had taken off towards the rapidly dispersing crowd. Sophia and Avery scrambled to catch up, as their little sister pressed on. Through an eclectic mix of people, from well-heeled ladies and gentlemen in fine coats, to working men in dusty shirts, the siblings pressed forward after their sister.

After clearing the crowd and making their way past the front of Federal Hall, Sophia and Avery followed Vera around a corner. They chased her up a narrow street, until they could see her stop ahead.

A door opened, and out stepped the men from the stage.

Vera stood, wide eyed and adorable, looking up and waving. Just as Avery and Sophia caught up, they heard her exclaim, "Hello George Washington!"

Panting and fighting for air, Avery and Sophia looked up to see, standing before them, President George Washington. He was taller than they expected, taller than most people they knew, certainly over 6 feet. Up close they could see that his clothes were nice but not flashy. From the silver buckles on his shoes to the steel handled sword at his waist, he looked every bit as dignified and impressive in the flesh as he did on the quarters in Avery's pocket.

Men circled around to get between the president and the unexpected interruption by three siblings from the future. Washington waved the men off, knelt down, and addressed the children very politely.

"Greetings my young Americans, what might your names be?"

Sophia was blown away, unable to muster any words at all. Luckily, Vera chimed in again.

"I'm Vera, and this is my sister Sophia, and my brother Avery." She chirped.

"Yes, um…your honor, the president sir," Avery managed to stammer out, blown away by the emotion of the moment.

"Ha! The innocence of youth. You may call me 'Mr. President' my dear children. Congress suggested more regal titles and honorifics but I declined. The presidency needs to be an office of service."

"Of course Mr. President," Sophia said, her mouth finally catching up with her amazement. "It is just so incredible to meet you. I mean, you're such a hero to all of us."

"I am touched by your words," he began, "but I have done no more than any man in my position would have."

"And it's so funny that we met you, because we were just captured by the British!" Avery blurted out. "And they said they were going to attack from Brooklyn, and they said we were spies for you, and…And…It was all just so crazy!"

This was met by a very confused look from George Washington, whose good nature won out as he moved towards Avery. "Well perhaps that information could have helped me in the Battle of Brooklyn, but it matters not my young lad," he said, giving Avery a pat on the head. "The war is over, and a new age of freedom and democracy has been born for all."

Avery blushed just a little, realizing what he had told the president may have already happened in the past, but that he and his siblings had moved forward in time since escaping the British soldiers. In any event, it was all pretty confusing.

"There is just so much we want to tell you, and ask you, and thank you for!" Sophia added.

"And I wish that there were time my young friends. I must be off to the chapel, for Congress has decided that it is important for the presidential inauguration to have ritual and routine. There are many things I must do today and from now on, in order to set precedents and lay the ground for the future."

The three siblings looked at each other and smiled, knowing that they have a secret, knowledge that the new president standing before them didn't. They knew how well he would do, knew that the fears that America had at the time all worked out, and they knew that President Washington most certainly would not let anyone down.

"Goodbye Mr. President!" the three say, almost in unison.

After George Washington and his entourage turned to walk away, the trio stood for a minute in silence, amazed by what had just happened and savoring the moment. Avery rubbed the quarters in his pocket, enjoying the new and special meaning they now had.

They turned away and looked at each other smiling, forgetting for a moment just how far they were from home. They had just stood at the birthplace of the presidency, with only them knowing how well it would go.

Part V

With all the excitement of meeting one of the great heroes of history, the children were practically floating with joy and excitement. While their time travelling adventures may have landed them in a little hot water, it was all worth it for that one experience.

They were so happy that they hadn't even noticed the once again, something had changed.

In fact, it wasn't a loud noise, a flash of light, or anything they saw that had alerted them to this newest transition; It was the *smell*.

"P.U." Vera said, waving her hand in front of her nose in an exaggerated manner, then looking at her brother.

"Hey!" Avery said, "I don't know what you're talking about."

"Oh man, I do" Sophia added, covering her own mouth and nose just as the smell caught up with Avery.

"Ok, that is pretty gross" Avery said to a now giggling Vera, amused by the joke she had made to her brother.

"What is it?" Vera asked, settling down enough to be genuinely curious.

"I'm not sure," Sophia offered. "Let's have a look."

The siblings stepped forward, out of the alley they had found themselves in. There were a few small rows of brownstones, the first buildings they had seen in a long time that actually looked somewhat familiar. Up ahead, stood a very large complex. Occupying an entire city block, it had a big marquee, and very ornate architecture. The neighborhood looked like it was still popping up, with empty spaces between some buildings, not quite as crowded as the city they knew.

Then, they figured out the source of the smell.

In the center of an open area were horses. Dozens of them. There were horses in corrals and horses walking the streets. There were lines of carriages, not unlike the ones they had seen earlier in Central Park, with some being used and others lined up like cars at a dealership. There were more horses in a single place than the children had ever seen.

"Horsies!" Vera squealed, delighting in being so close to the beautiful animals once again. Having acclimated to the randomness of time travel, she seemed to be embracing whatever came next.

"So now we know what a hundred horses smell like" Sophia declared.

"And it isn't pretty," Avery added.

The children set about exploring further. As they walked into the open square in the middle of everything, they were amazed by what they saw. Between the smaller homes and the giant buildings were small shops with striped awnings, finally *beginning* to resemble things they knew from their own time.

"Look at that!" Avery said, pointing up at the side of a large building.

In giant metal letters, adorning the side of the structure was the word "Heinz" inside of a pickle shape. Under it was the statement "57 Good Things For The Table: Preserves, India Relish, Malt Vinegar, Tomato Chutney, Sweet Pickles." It wasn't quite a billboard like they had seen in modern New York, but it was a lot closer than a field full of corn.

"Wow!" Sophia exclaimed. "And look, there's more!"

As the children looked around they saw lettering painted on the sides of many buildings. There were advertisements for a building developments called "Tangiers: Long Island" and a place called Bergen Beach. More lettering encouraged them to attend variety shows and visit opera companies.

"You know what this reminds me of?" Sophia added, asking mainly herself. "A lot of the buildings near the Broadway theaters have things written on them like this. They're usually really faded and peeling, but you can see that a long time ago there was something there!"

"Maybe this *is* that 'long time ago!'" Avery exclaimed, catching on.

The children were excited, finally feeling like they recognized something, and sensing that they may be that much closer to their parents and their own time. Suddenly, they were approached by a small boy.

"Not from around here, are you?" He said, not knowing the half of it.

"Well, not really. It's kind of complicated," Avery replied. "What's your name?"

"Danny. I'm pleased to meet you."

"Hi Danny. I'm Avery, and these are my sisters Sophia and Vera. Nice to meet you too."

He was no George Washington, but Avery was excited to meet a boy who seemed to be about his own age, and the girls were excited that they might have met someone with some answers.

"Looking for something?" Danny asked.

"Actually we're looking for our parents," Sophia replied.

"Ah, I understand " Danny said, "My own father is just over there; we sell carriages together. It's very exciting work; I get to meet all sorts of interesting people, like you three. I was sitting over there wondering to myself just where you might be from, with those funny looking clothes and all."

"Funny looking?" Avery said in disbelief. "This is getting a little old; I think we look pretty good."

"Apologies, I meant no offense" Danny was quick to reply. "It's just that I've met men and women from all parts, from Africa, all over Europe, even from China... and none of them dressed like you three."

Danny's own clothes were like something out of a movie. He wore a smart cap, along with grey trousers, a messy white shirt, and a vest. Like the kind of boy who sells newspapers on a street corner in pictures of old New York.

"Where are we?" Vera asked, always the one to cut quickly to the point.

"Why this is Longacre Square, a great place to visit on your first time in New York City!" Danny replied.

"Longacre Square?" Avery said quizzically, "I've never heard of that."

"Well let me explain for you out of towners," Danny started. "Longacre Square is the best place in New York City to buy a horse or carriage. It used to be all farms here, but lately a lot of new buildings have been put up. My pop says that they named it after Long Acre in London, which is the horse and carriage district there."

"Ah, so that's where the smell is coming from" Avery said.

"Hahaha," Danny laughed. "I suppose it does take some getting used to."

"So this is where they sell horses in New York City?" Sophia asked, and then added "What is that big building over there with all the signs on it?"

Sophia pointed to the large building with the marquee they had spotted earlier.

"Oh that? That's the new Olympia Theater. A Gentleman named Oscar Hammerstein put it up not long ago. Inside it has got three theaters, and they put on all sorts of shows. Operas, ballet, variety shows; it's changing the whole neighborhood."

"Theater?" Avery asked. "Is that the only theater around here?"

"Used to be," Danny replied, "but not anymore. Seems they just keep building them. There's the Lyceum and a few more that just opened. They do that big light show over on Broadway; some folks have taken to calling it the 'Great White Way.' It'll never catch on if you ask me."

Sophia and Avery swapped a knowing gaze, starting to catch on.

"Yup, the neighborhood is really changing. You see that big building starting to go up over there?" Danny asked, pointing.

The three siblings turned their heads to see the steel skeleton of a large building starting to rise up above the brownstones around it. The steel girders must have gone up hundreds of feet into the air.

"That there is a new skyscraper," Danny continued. "Gonna be the headquarters for the New York Times newspaper. Seems to be the way things are going around here - less and less about the horses and more about the big buildings."

"Wait a minute!" Sophia exclaimed, finally feeling a sense of where she was.

"The New York Times..." Avery started.

"And Broadway! This must be Times Square!" Sophia said, finishing his thought.

"We're so close now! Thank you so much Danny" Avery said, so grateful for the information their new friend had shared.

"Thanks!" Vera added, throwing her arms around Danny for a big hug.

"You're quite welcome. Best of luck to you Sophia, Avery, and Vera. I hope you find your parents and wherever it is you're headed."

Danny took off his cap and gave a courteous bow to the trio before turning and walking back towards the horses. The children once again took a chance to observe the scene.

They saw the big theatre and the advertisements in a new light. It really wasn't so different than the Times Square they knew, just a sort of beginning to it. There were places to shop and a lot of signs, just nothing neon and no screens full of video. The dusty dirt roads had no cars on them, but were still busy, or what must have been considered busy for the time period they were in.

"So if this is Times Square, that means we must be back in Manhattan!" Avery pointed out. "Should we try to find our way back to Central Park?"

"I'm not sure," Sophia replied. "It still doesn't solve the problem of being in the wrong century."

"Good point," Avery agreed.

"Yeah!" Vera chimed in, not knowing what the word century meant, but still bursting with energy despite the long journey.

"But," Sophia started, "I know we were planning on visiting Times Square with our family."

"You're right!" Avery exclaimed. "On the last day of our trip!"

"Yeah" Vera giggled, making a game out of agreeing.

"We need to figure out how to get home, and fast." Sophia said.

Just then, a big crowd started to filter out of what the children now understood to be the Olympia complex. A show must have just ended. Stepping out into the midday sun, men put back on their hats and took arms with women as they spread out over the square. Seemingly oblivious to the three children standing there, the crowd began pushing the children towards Broadway.

"Excuse me!" Vera exclaimed, stepping out of the way of adults who seemed not to even notice the siblings existed.

Sophia, Avery, and Vera kept sidestepping to get out of the way of the crowd, staying close together, instinctively preparing themselves for something to happen. It occurred to them that each time they got lost in a crowd; they seemed to pop up in a new time and place.

Finally, the children stopped fighting it, grabbed each other tight and let the crowd surround them, preparing for the next leg of their journey…

Epilogue

As the crowd around them finally dispersed, the trio opened their eyes. Without knowing it, they had all instinctively shut their eyes tight, in expectation of another time travelling adventure. Where would they be now?

But nothing had changed.

The three of them looked around, trying to see what had happened. Were they surrounded by soldiers again, or about to meet some great historical figure? No. They were still standing at the edge of the square, still smelling horses, and still no closer to home.

"This can't be!" Avery exclaimed, sure that something should have changed.

"Shouldn't we have time travelled again?" Sophia asked. "Maybe this is a different square, or a different year, or a different *something*, right?"

Just then the three of them looked over to see Danny, their carriage selling friend, waving to them, before turning back to fasten a wheel to a large black buggy.

"No, I think nothing happened this time," Avery conceded. "Last time we disappeared in a crowd we met George Washington!"

"Right," Sophia replied. "And remember before that, when we met Nathaniel Lord Britton? He was so nice to us."

"And the concert in Central Park" Vera added, dancing in place to emphasize the experience.

"Don't forget being captured by British troops," Avery added.

"Don't worry, I won't!" Sophia replied.

"And the really loud noises from the men who were breaking the rocks!" Vera exclaimed, still referring to their time exploring the early days of Central Park.

"You're right. We have so many stories to share, I want to get back to tell our family about all the fun we've had more than anything else." Sophia explained.

"Me too!" Avery exclaimed. "I can't believe we really met him," as he pulled one of the quarters from his pocket to show his sisters.

The "him" Avery was referring to was, of course, George Washington.

"And the robot!" Vera added, still having fun listing their adventures.

"Wait a second! The robot!" Sophia practically shouted, having a moment of clarity. "That's when this all started, with the man who was dressed like a robot; the man in Central Park!"

"Well sure, but don't blame me for it" Avery said. "He was just doing some really cool moves."

"No one is blaming you." Sophia clarified. "I think you can save us! I think I know how to get home."

With that Sophia gave her brother a big hug, and grabbed the quarter from his hand.

"This all started when you dropped a quarter in the robot's hat in the park. Maybe that's how we can get back!" Sophia explained.

"Yay!" Vera shouted.

"Good thinking sis," Avery added.

Sophia quickly scanned the square, spotting a lone man on the street corner with an accordion. He was playing and singing a sad, slow song, and had a hat at his feet to collect donations.

"Follow me!" Sophia declared.

The children approached the musician, his bittersweet melody not exactly lifting anyone's spirits. Sophia held up the quarter for him to see, and slowly placed it in the hat.

The sight of the quarter, which the trio realized was a lot more money a hundred years ago than it is today, perked up the lonely musician, who quickly changed his tune. A big smile came over his face as he launched into a happy song, whose upbeat tempo had the children clapping and dancing for joy.

As they enjoyed the music, a whooshing sound came over the square, and all of it was just overwhelming enough to distract them for a split second.

"Sophia!? Avery!? Vera!?" a familiar voice called out. "Helloooo?"

The trio turned to see their mother and father standing just behind them, followed by their older siblings.

"There you are," their mother continued. "Are you ready to take the picture?"

The three turned to each other, then looked around. There they were, in the middle of Times Square again. Only this time, it was covered in bright billboards, neon lights, and giant displays. Car horns honked all around them, and people in modern clothes dashed about.

They had made it back.

"I turn my back for one second..." their father started. "Time to get back over here for the photo."

As the family of eight gathered around to have their photo taken by a friendly tourist, the three siblings looked at each other, confused. One second? Had no one noticed how long they were gone? Had they even really been gone? What had happened to them?

"Cheese!" they all said, smiling as the camera flashed.

"Oh and here Sophia, you dropped this," said their mother, handing her a quarter.

As Sophia turned to give the coin back to her brother, they both looked down at the image of George Washington, who they still swear to this day, was winking at them.

The End

Appendix A: Alternate Activities

Many spend their whole lives in New York City and do not get to experience so much of what it has to provide. There are so many great activities that were not included in the main itinerary presented in this book, not because they don't have a lot to offer - but because time, location, and other logistics did not permit.

Alternately, while we have done our best to create a trip that will appeal to many families, tastes vary and priorities are different from person to person.

The following represents a cross-section of RealFamilyTrips.com's "best of the rest", in the form of activities, locations, and excursions that didn't make the cut for the main text of this book. In most cases, we will note why they were ultimately not included. In all cases we indicate where they would best fit.

If you find anything in the main portion of this book unappealing to you, look here to "swap something out" for an option that better suits your family. If you like more (or less) action, here is where you can find alternate ideas to customize a trip for your family.

Also, if you plan on spending more than 7 days in New York City, you can expand upon our original itinerary by adding from this section.

Your vacation is about your family. Make sure that what you plan to do represents the best possible choices for you and your children. Alternate activities have been arranged by borough for easier browsing.

Manhattan

The Statue of Liberty

Why We Omitted It: The trip out to Liberty Island takes time, and means sacrificing a decent chunk of touring opportunity. While there is information to learn on the island, and fun to be had climbing the statue, we opted to design the main itinerary in a manner that allows you to see and experience more. We also made sure to allow for opportunities for great views of The Statue of Liberty from Battery Park, the Staten Island Ferry, the speedboat ride, and assorted other stops. Our goal was to maximize your time during the day in lower Manhattan, and to allow you to experience all five boroughs. By no means did we mean to minimize the importance of this site.

Where it Goes: Easiest to fit in on Day 5 in lower Manhattan.

Perhaps New York City's single most recognizable and famous landmark, the Statue of Liberty (officially, *Liberty En-*

lightening the World) is a neoclassical sculpture gifted to the United States by France and dedicated in 1886. The vision of French sculptor Frédéric Auguste Bartholdi, the statue was constructed by Gustave Eiffel (whose eponymous tower adorns Paris). The torch bearing arm and head were completed ahead of the rest of the statue, and were displayed at international expositions, including one in Philadelphia in 1876, in part to raise money for the rest of the statue and the pedestal required to display it. The statue was completed, and its dedication presided over by President Grover Cleveland, ending in New York City's first ever ticker tape parade.

Fun Fact: The tablet held by "Lady Liberty" bears an inscription of the Declaration of Independence. Another detail of the statue which is often overlooked are the broken chains which lay at her feet.

The robed woman the statue depicts is the Roman goddess Libertas, and its creation after the American Civil War was actually a testament to the abolition of slavery, rather than the open immigration policies of the United States. It was originally proposed by French political philosopher Édouard René de Laboulaye, who believed that the Union victory during the Civil War represented the notions of true freedom and democracy becoming a reality in the United States, and that recognition of these ideals should be a joint international effort.

The history of the statue is fascinating, and ever since it has appeared on US ground, it has stood as a symbol of the American Dream. Its placement in New York Harbor (though it is actually closer to New Jersey, the federal land is administered by New York State) has allowed it to serve as a "welcome sign" for millions of immigrants and a symbol of new beginnings.

Travel Tip: According to the National Parks Department, to enjoy both Ellis and Liberty Islands in the same day, with enough time to see most of what you would want to, you should plan to be on a Statue Cruises Ferry that departs from Battery Park or Liberty State Park before 1:00 PM. Given how busy things can get during the peak travel periods, we recommend arriving even earlier.

Visiting the statue may be a time consuming proposition, but once you arrive at Liberty Island your journey will be rewarded. We recommend that you reserve tickets in advance, as this is a very busy spot, especially in the spring and summer. It is well worth the extra time and money to visit the crown, after investing the time making it to the island. For the crown, reservations are required. From the scenic and enjoyable ferry ride, to the informative park ranger-led tours, to the views from the top, and the idea of standing at the feet of Lady Liberty herself - a trip to the Statue of Liberty is a wonderful experience for families who take the time to venture there.

Address: Liberty Island, New York, NY

NYC Ferry Terminal - 1 Battery Place, New York, New York 10004

New Jersey Ferry Terminal - 1 Audrey Zapp Drive, Jersey City, New Jersey 07305

Phone: (212) 363-3200 (Park), 1-877-523-9849 (Ferry)

Hours: First ferry departs mainland at 8:30 AM (last one at 5 PM). Last return ferry from Liberty Island departs 6:45 PM. Ferries are busy during peak months (April - September) and wait times can be up to 90 minutes during that time. Also allow time to pass through security and note that the island begins shutting down 30 minutes prior to the last ferry. Open every day of the year except December 25.

Website: www.nps.gov/stli/index.htm (Park), www.statuecruises.com (Ferry)

Approximate Cost: Ferry fee (includes pedestal access and tour by a ranger) Adults (13+) $18, Children (4-12) $9, Children under 4 are FREE. Crown access is an additional $3 for ages 4 and up; under 4 not allowed.

Approximate Length: Varies with season (as you may have to wait for a ferry) but including a round trip and time to tour, expect anywhere from **2-5 hours** for just Liberty Island, at least half a day for both Liberty and Ellis Islands, up to a whole day.

Ellis Island

Why We Omitted It: The trip out to Ellis Island takes time (though it makes much more sense to go see Ellis Island if you decide to see the Statue of Liberty), and means sacrificing a decent chunk of touring time. You have a chance to at least see it from afar (and not so far) during stops at Battery Park, the Staten Island Ferry, the speedboat ride, and assorted other stops. Our goal was to maximize your time during the day in lower Manhattan, and to allow you to experience all five boroughs. By no means did we mean to minimize the importance of this site.

Where it Goes: Easiest to fit in on Day 5 in lower Manhattan.

From 1892 to 1954, Ellis Island served as the literal and figurative gateway to the American dream. This immigration inspection station was among the busiest in the United States, and over 12 million individuals began their new lives as Americans on this tiny island in New York Harbor. The site now houses a premier (and free) museum to the immigrant experience, documenting the process of naturalizing at Ellis Island, as well as the stories of particular individuals with a chance to explore records and perform research.

Travel Tip: According to the National Parks Department, to enjoy both Ellis and Liberty Islands in the same day, with enough time to see most of what you would want to, you should plan to be on a Statue Cruises Ferry that departs from Battery Park or Liberty State Park before 1:00 PM. Given how busy things can get during the peak travel periods, we recommend arriving even earlier.

Three different floors in the museum display important artifacts from the immigration experience, including historical photographs, luggage carried on the journey to America, antique news clippings, political cartoons, and accounts from famous immigrants. This museum is an immersive experience, walking you through the same areas so many men and women stood, eagerly awaiting their chance to "make it" in the new world. One of the major goals of the facility is to stress the sacrifice made to get to America. Here, parents will find valuable lessons to teach their children, and form deeper connections to ancestors and a respect for the gifts of the American experience.

One of the other benefits of a visit to Ellis Island is the opportunity to perform personal **research.** The island houses a vast database, and all visitors are welcome to research their own ancestors and seek out names, dates, and other details about their family members that may be difficult to find elsewhere. This can be another great opportunity for families, whether it be making progress on a project to research your family tree, or the opportunity to show your children firsthand where they come from and what it took to make their lives possible.

The Immigration Wall of Honor memorial bears over 700,000 names of families with ties to Ellis Island. Take time to look and feel the weight of history, and to see if your family name is somewhere on the wall. Ranger led tours of the museum are free, and last approximately 30 minutes. There is also the option (for ages 13 and older) to take a 90 minute hard hat tour of the 750 bed Ellis Island Hospital facility for an additional fee. Here you walk in the footsteps of immigrants in an even more immersive way, standing in hospital rooms, a laundry facility, staff quarters, and other rooms that were used to treat the sick as they tried to get well enough to be admitted to the country. There is also an art exhibit, "Unframed - Ellis Island," which uses life sized paintings and cutouts to put you toe to toe with "immigrants" and "staff" and set the stage for the locations you will visit. We advise reserving tickets, which can be done through the same company that runs the ferry.

Travel Tip: While there are food options on the island, they are limited and have the luxury of being able to charge what they want. We advise grabbing a bite before getting here, to save time and money. Also, security checks mean that bags will slow you down, and are best left behind if not absolutely needed.

With unique opportunities for research, and special insight into the past, Ellis Island is a very different kind of museum. This is a place where a family can feel a special connection to their heritage, and hopefully, to each other as well.

Address: Ellis Island, New York, NY

NYC Ferry Terminal - 1 Battery Place, New York, New York 10004

New Jersey Ferry Terminal - 1 Audrey Zapp Drive, Jersey City, New Jersey 07305

Phone: (212)561-4588 (Museum), 1-877-523-9849 (Ferry)

Hours: Museum open from 9:30 AM - 5:15 PM. First ferry departs mainland at 8:30 AM (last one at 5 PM). Last return ferry from Liberty Island departs 7:00 PM. Ferries are busy during peak months (April - September) and wait times can be up to 90 minutes during that time. Also allow time to pass through security and note that the island begins shutting down 30 minutes prior to the last ferry. Open every day of the year except December 25.

Website: www.nps.gov/elis/index.htm (Park/Museum), www.statuecruises.com (Ferry)

Approximate Cost: Ferry fee (includes museum access and tour by a ranger) Adults (13+) $18, Children (4-12) $9, Children under 4 are FREE. Hospital tours are an additional $25 for ages 13 and up, under 13 not allowed.

Approximate Length: Varies with season (as you may have to wait for a ferry) but including a round trip and time to tour, expect anywhere from **2-5 hours** for just Ellis Island, at least half a day for both Ellis and Liberty Islands, up to a whole day.

The Metropolitan Museum of Art

Why We Omitted It: Art exhibits are featured at several of the stops in the main itinerary, including Snug Harbor, Lenny's Creations, and the chance to pop into galleries in SoHo, to name a few. The "Met" (as it is affectionately known) is a fantastic museum and well worth the visit, however for the main itinerary we chose to focus on museums that offered interactivity or other options to engage younger children. If your children are older, or particularly interested in art, this is a great place to swap in.

Where it Goes: Midtown Manhattan, either day 1 or 7.

With over 2 million works divided among 17 departments, and one of the largest museum buildings by area in the world, the Metropolitan Museum of Art is a sprawling mecca to the fine arts across a variety of disciplines. Founded in 1870, the largest art museum in the United States is still committed to the same mission it was way back then: bringing the highest quality art and art education to the American people.

The museum's eclectic offerings span the history of the modern world, and present the wide variety of visual forms through which human beings have expressed themselves. There are the expected paintings and sculptures, representing priceless works from all the major European "masters" that define our classic notion of art. Also present are American and modern works that show the progression of the art world.

At the same time, you will find extensive collections from a variety of world cultures, including African, Asian, Oceanic, Byzantine, and Islamic art. Exhibits span back to ancient Egypt and classical antiquity, tracing the roots of visual forms back to some of their earliest known examples. The collection is rounded out by unique offerings that will expand your family's knowledge and impress upon you that art and expression are not limited to typical gallery holdings, with extensive collections of musical instruments, costumes, accessories, weapons and armor from around the world.

The extensive offerings of the museum are a boon to visitors, but can also be a bit intimidating for families if you don't visit with a plan in mind. You could easily spend days on end here, still not managing to see it all. On a busy trip to New York City, and with children in tow, it is best to select a few key exhibits to ensure everyone remains engaged and that there is still time to see more.

Travel Tip: There is an online map that can be compared to the list of exhibitions, in order to determine what sounds best to your family and where it is. There is also an app that you can download for free (available on iOS and Android) that allows you to view a map and information on the exhibits. Download it in advance of your trip to research and build excitement, then use it while in the museum to help you get around.

We have our own recommendations for families, with two particular exhibits that will excite children and expand their image of what a museum has to offer:

1. **Arms and Armor** - takes a look into the history of the equipment warriors carried into battle throughout the ages. From medieval knights to Japanese samurais, this exhibit focuses the exquisite craftsmanship and intricate artwork that adorned classical armor and weaponry. Appropriate for all ages, this exhibit is a great way to get children excited, as they stand toe to toe with elaborate artifacts from the past. They may also be surprised by how much shorter people were back then, and leave thinking they could have squeezed into one of those suits themselves!

2. **The Temple of Dendur** - is an Egyptian temple from the Roman Era reign of Augustus Caesar, completed around 10 BC. The religious building is a relatively small example of such a structure, devoted to the Egyptian god Isis. Awarded to the Metropolitan Museum of Art in 1967, the structure was painstakingly disassembled and transported across the Atlantic Ocean, where it was reassembled inside the Sackler Wing of the museum for visitors to enjoy. You can actually step inside the temple (its sandstone walls are protected by plexiglass shields) and observe the ancient carvings up close and personal, standing in the footsteps of ancient Egyptians while still inside the museum. This is a real winner for children, and a chance to feel transported to a faraway land while still remaining comfortably on Fifth Avenue.

These are just our suggestions, and whether you chose to see these, or take in any of the other highlights of the extensive collection, any visit to "The Met" (as locals call it) is sure to be a great experience for any family.

Address: 1000 5th Ave, New York, NY 10028

Phone: (212) 535-7710 (Customer Service), (212) 535-7710 (Tickets)

Email: mettours@metmuseum.org

Hours: Sunday - Thursday, 10 AM - 5:30 PM. Thursday & Friday, 10 AM - 9 PM.

Website: www.metmuseum.org/

Approximate Cost: Adults (13+), $25. Students, $12. Children (under 12) FREE. Tickets can be purchased online. **NOTE:** This price includes same-week admission to The Cloisters, see next alternate stop for more information. All prices are suggested, and if you choose to, you can pay less.

Approximate Length: We advise spending **90 minutes to 2 hours** here with children, depending on what other stops you are willing to change to enjoy this museum.

The Cloisters

Why We Omitted It: The uptown location is out of the way of other stops on the suggested itinerary, but a quick subway ride will make it more than accessible for you and your family.

Where it Goes: Easiest from one of the midtown Manhattan Days, 1 or 7.

Often overlooked by tourists and native New Yorkers alike, this museum operated by the Metropolitan Museum of Art is a real treat hidden in the north of the city. Located in Fort Tryon Park, The Cloisters features impressive medieval architecture, which houses some amazing works of art.

Its out of the way location and quiet nature make it ideal for families who want to avoid the thickest crowds and loudest noise. Besides the impressive collection, one of the real joys of visiting is the fact that the museum is perched on a hill overlooking the Hudson River. You will have a stunning view of the granite cliffs across the river and the boats on the water, and if visiting in spring or summer, the stunning gardens will be perfect for a thoughtful gaze, or a relaxing stroll.

Travel Tip: Download a PDF map of The Cloisters in advance of your visit to help plan.

The Cloisters represents the wing of the Metropolitan Museum of Art dedicated to medieval European art and architecture. Opened in 1938, the main museum building is a fascinating amalgamation of different elements from the past. Rather than copying a specific building, the designers borrowed elements from a variety of ecclesiastical and secular standards, to create a structure that portrays a variety of styles and arranges them in chronological order. This building-as-an-exhibit feature adopts elements from such actual medieval cloisters as Saint-Michel-de-Cuxa, Saint-Guilhem-le-Désert, Trie-sur-Baïse, Froville, and Bonnefont-en-Comminges. It affords a special opportunity to examine years of architecture and span the continent of Europe in just a few steps.

Inside you'll find an extensive collection of paintings, tapestries, sculptures, and more, made possible by the generosity of such notables as the famous John D. Rockefeller. Some of the more famous pieces include The Belles Heures of Jean de France, Duc de Berry, a carved ivory cross from a 12th century English abbey, and stained-glass windows from the castle chapel at Ebreichsdorf, Austria.

The collection is amazing, and the architecture stunning. You and your children will feel like you are touring a castle nestled into the western edge of Washington Heights. The experience includes the ability to take in the grounds, and you can make a great afternoon out of grabbing lunch and eating in the park, before or after wandering the facility at your own pace.

Address: 99 Margaret Corbin Dr, New York, NY 10040

Phone: (212) 923-3700

Hours: Open Daily except Thanksgiving, Christmas and New Year's Day. March - October, 10 AM - 5:15 PM. November - February, 10 AM - 4:45 PM.

Website: www.metmuseum.org/visit/visit-the-cloisters

Approximate Cost: Adults $25, Seniors $17, Students (with ID) $12, Children under 12 Free. Tickets can be purchased online. **NOTE:** Includes admission to the Metropolitan Museum of Art/included if you already purchased admission to the Met. See previous alternate stop for more information.

Approximate Length: We recommend spending **an hour or so** here, possibly longer if you stop for food or to sit in the park.

Afternoon Tea at the Plaza Hotel

Why We Omitted It: Our main itinerary features more ideas for sightseeing and educational activities, but this is a great option for the family that is feeling a bit rushed and wants to slow things down. It is also a great option in case the weather gets bad, to swap in for time in a park or one of the boat rides in order to stay dry.

Where it Goes: Any of the Manhattan days, though easiest on a midtown day, 1 or 7.

While English style high tea may be decidedly more London than New York City, this opportunity to enjoy old fashioned New York elegance at one of its most famous landmarks is a great addition to any family vacation. The iconic, castle-like building occupies a choice stretch facing Central Park and offers some of the best in modern amenities coupled with old world class.

The famous building has long been a favorite for visiting celebrities and dignitaries. Over the course of its storied history, it was the place that The Beatles stayed during their first visit to the United States, Miles Davis recorded an album in the hotel's Persian Room, and Truman Capote hosted his famous "Black and White Ball" in the Grand Ballroom. The Plaza Accord was an agreement among international finance ministers of developed countries negotiated and signed at the hotel in 1985. On a lighter note, it was also the center of the famous antics of "Home Alone 2" as one fictional child made New York City his playground.

Travel Tip: Besides tea here, consider tours offered by the hotel to the public, to take in the history and opulence of the building itself.

Afternoon tea in the famous Palm Court will allow you to sit under a stunning stained glass dome. Enjoy world class service with the finest china and linens, along with a tea list of international pedigree, and fun foods that kids will love.

This stop can offer a great change of pace, whether you use it to take a break from the hustle and bustle, brighten a rainy day, or simply to enjoy some world class service in a setting that will be sure to amaze everyone back home.

Address: 768 5th Ave, New York, NY 10019

Phone: (212) 759-3000

Hours: Tea service runs 12:30 PM - 4:30 PM.

Website: www.theplazany.com/dining/palmcourt/

Approximate Cost: $31 to $50, easiest to book via OpenTable.

Approximate Length: About **1 hour** or so.

Madame Tussaud's Wax Museum

Why We Omitted It: While a fun stop for families, this stop is not unique to New York (Madame Tussaud's has other locations, and there are similar wax museums worldwide). We favored things that can only be done in New York City or that had a distinct flair to distinguish them.

Where it Goes: Easiest to fit in on day 7, though it could also work on day 1 in midtown Manhattan.

Madame Tussaud's is world famous and a NYC highlight since the year 2000, while their London outpost dates back 200 years and all locations can trace their roots back to 18th century France. The realistic wax figures of individuals ranging from celebrities, to fictional characters, and world leaders will amaze young and old alike.

Madame Tussaud herself learned the art of wax sculpture in Paris during the 1770's, serving as art tutor to King Louis XVI's sister at the Palace of Versailles. She survived the chaos of the French Revolution, bringing her art and her talents to Great Britain at the beginning of the 19th century. In an age before ubiquitous photography and video, her sculptures brought news and culture to life in a way few people had ever experienced before. While the art form may seem dated at this point, there is still a special charm to standing side by side with life sized replicas of individuals we have known, admired, or imagined from afar.

They are constantly adding new figures as their ever growing collection expands to offer something for every member of the family. From entertainment classics like Charlie Chaplin and Marilyn Monroe for parents, to Marvel superheroes and pop sensations for children and teens, this Times Square space packs a lot into your ticket. Experience the figures and interactive exhibits, which include areas dedicated to Pop Culture, Film & TV, a Sports Zone, and "The Spirit of New York" - an exhibit that takes you inside some of the city's most famous people and neighborhoods to frame your New York City vacation in a unique way.

Download the app for a preview of your experience. Take memorable family photos with your favorite "stars" (or at least their wax doubles) and enjoy what millions of tourists each year know as one of New York's most visited attractions.

Address: 234 W 42nd Street New York, NY, right in the heart of Times Square

Phone: (212) 512-9600

Hours: Opening Times Vary 9 - 10 AM, Closing Time Between 3 PM and 10 PM. See schedule to plan your trip.

Website: www.madametussauds.com/NewYork/

Approximate Cost: Adults from $29.70, Children from $24 (Buy Tickets Online & Save up to 20%).

Approximate Length: We recommend **1-2 hours** here.

Chelsea Piers

Why We Omitted It: The activities here are a lot of fun, and while they offer a distinct twist and great New York City setting, they are not entirely different from similar things you could experience elsewhere, or at home. If you want to get a bit more active or cut loose and have some fun - we say go for it. Our main itinerary is just more focused on uniquely New York activities.

Where it Goes: Day 5, lower Manhattan.

Chelsea Piers is a massive complex in the Manhattan neighborhood of the same name, occupying a wonderful stretch of waterfront and serving up a unique blend of sport, games, event space, and great activities for people of all ages.

There is a remarkable array of different facilities within this stretch of piers west of 11th Avenue. There is the Sports Complex, which offers a health club, day spa, the city's largest gymnastics training center, two basketball courts, indoor fields for lacrosse and soccer, batting cages, a rock climbing wall, and dance studios. The Golf Club features a huge, multi-story driving range, looking out over the Hudson River. That is just scratching the surface of the many offerings here, at a facility that serves New Yorkers and tourists alike.

The land now occupied by Chelsea Piers was once a functioning terminal for ships. It was from here that Jesse Owens and the 1936 Summer Olympic team departed for the games of Berlin, Germany. The original piers were built in reaction to the booming luxury line business of 1910 on through the 30's, when the city actually took away a block of land that was once a part of Manhattan to create larger waterfront structures. The great ships of that day docked here, including the RMS Lusitania. These piers were actually the destination of the RMS Titanic.

When the 1930's arrived, the development of even larger ships required further action on the part of the city. It was at this time that the New York Cruise Terminal between West 46th and West 54th Street was created (which is where today's cruise ships still dock) and eventually the downtown piers fell out of use. In 1994, construction began on the modern facilities that exist here today, and the repurposing is a terrific example of the way in which New York City continues to reinvent itself, and push the same small amount of land to new and exciting heights.

There are so many options here for families, but to help narrow things down, we recommend the following activities:

1. **Bowling at Bowlmor Lanes** - The sleek and modern facilities at Bowlmor offer something for all ages. Enjoy a game or two, and if you like, a bite to eat. This is a great activity that doesn't take too long, and that parents and children can enjoy equally. [**Contact Info:** Pier 62, Suite 300 - 23rd St. & Hudson River Park - (212) 336-6777]

2. **Sail on the Schooner America 2.0** - This 105 foot vessel offer plenty of room to spread out on chartered sails around New York Harbor, that take advantage of some of the few remaining, functional piers located at the facility. Set sail for a fun afternoon, from the same port that launched some of history's greatest ships, with an array of fun activities and options for all tastes. [**Contact Info:** Chelsea Piers, Suite 103 New York, NY 10011 - (212) 913-9991]

3. **Pier 62 Skatepark** - The Pier 62 Skateboard Park is a place where skateboarders of all ages can practice their skills and learn new tricks. The park includes an Ollie Zone for beginners, an Ollie Ledge that spans 18 feet, and an Intermediate Fun Box for more advanced skaters and boarders. [**Contact Info:** Pier 62 at Chelsea Piers New York, NY 10011 - (212) 242-6427]

Whatever you choose to do at Chelsea Piers, you are sure to find something to suit your family's needs. Kick things up a notch with a nice variety of fun and activity, or slow things down with some spa time and a great meal. Meet kids on their level with activities they love, and enjoy a great venue that allows you to savor New York City views while enjoying the things you love to do.

Address: 62 Chelsea Piers, New York, NY 10011

Phone: (212) 336-6666

Hours: Main facility open daily from 6:30 AM - Midnight. Hours for individual activities vary.

Website: www.chelseapiers.com/

Approximate Cost: Varies with the activities you select.

Approximate Length: Also varies a lot depending on what you choose to do. You could spend an hour here or a whole day, just decide how many other stops you are willing to eliminate and choose activities accordingly.

Chelsea Market

Why We Omitted It: Grabbing food along the way allows more time for touring. If you are looking for a destination meal, or choose to wind your way towards Chelsea Piers, this is a great option.

Where it Goes: Day 5, lower Manhattan.

This charming downtown market is a modern facility housed in a gorgeous old building. The indoor market and shopping center has a lot of charm and doesn't feel like a more commercial mall.

This square block of market space houses over 35 vendors, in an area that has long been an epicenter of food culture in New York City. For the Algonquin Indians, this spot near the river was a central place from which to trade crops and game. As part of the meatpacking district, during the days of the thriving butcher trade, the trains of the High Line served as a shady overhang, under which wholesale meat vendors cooled their wares with large blocks of Hudson River ice. Eventually, the National Biscuit Company built a factory on this block in the 19th century, in order to take advantage of the lard easily available from these local butchers.

The cracker factory long since closed, the renovated space has been reinvented as an indoor market visited by some 6 million people every year. The bare brick and industrial finishes lend unique charm to the space. A great representation of the gentrification of the neighborhood it resides in, Chelsea Market represents the evolution of the New York City food scene.

There are a number of quaint shops and places to eat. This is a great place to grab a midday meal and maybe knock off a little souvenir shopping at the same time. It will keep kids entertained as well, as you wander past many of the small, engaging merchants. Watch bread be made or cupcakes iced outside a glass walled bakery, or see some exotic handmade basketry. True foodies will also enjoy that the upper floor of this building houses studios for The Food Network, and you might just catch a glimpse of a celebrity chef on their way to work! Check the schedule to see special events that may coincide with your visit.

Address: 75 9th Ave, New York, NY 10011

Phone: (212) 652-2110

Hours: Monday - Saturday 7 AM - 9 PM, Sunday 8 AM - 8 PM.

Website: www.chelseamarket.com/

Approximate Cost: Free to explore, food varies by location.

Approximate Length: About a **half hour** to eat, up to an **hour** to wander as well.

The Museum of Modern Art (MoMa)

Why We Omitted It: Modern art isn't for everyone, and in an effort to make our main itinerary as universally appealing as possible, we opted to include this in the alternate activities. If your family is at all interested, or curious, about the modern art scene - go for it.

Where it Goes: Any of the Manhattan Days, 1, 5 or 7.

To the art world, MoMa is viewed as one of the most influential museums of modern art in the world - helping to define and shape just what art means today. For families, it is a unique glimpse into an often mystifying world, and a chance to see a healthy mix of the familiar and the decidedly new - for an experience best enjoyed when starting with an open mind and a curious demeanor.

The history of the museum dates back to Abby Aldrich Rockefeller (wife of John D. Rockefeller) who, along with two of her friends came to be known as *"the daring ladies."* The ladies came up with the vision for a space that would lend exposure and credence to the modern art scene by sharing it with the public at large. Nine days after the market crash of 1929, they opened their first space in the Heckscher Building at 730 Fifth Avenue. What began in a small rented room grew over the years, to eventually include a famous Vincent van Gogh exhibit in 1935, and a Picasso retrospective from 1939-40 that would help the effort gain international prominence. Over the years the museum and its holdings grew, eventually resulting in the current space, designed by famed architect Yoshio Taniguchi and opening its doors in 2004.

The museum has an impressive collection that spans the incredible variety of media that makes up modern art. There are paintings, drawings, designs, prints and photography - in addition to sculpture, architecture, video, and other electronic media. Some of the more famous works here include:

- Vincent van Gogh, The Starry Night
- Andy Warhol, Campbell's Soup Cans
- Pablo Picasso, Les Demoiselles d'Avignon
- Claude Monet, Water Lilies triptych
- Jasper Johns, Flag
- Frida Kahlo, Self-Portrait With Cropped Hair
- Paul Cézanne, The Bather
- Marc Chagall, I and the Village
- Salvador Dalí, The Persistence of Memory

Travel Tip: Like some other museums, MoMa has an app that allows you to take a look at the collection, find your way around the museum and get excited for your trip. It is currently only available for iOS.

View the calendar to see what events are currently going on, as well as the current temporary exhibits. You can also explore the museum online to find what areas interest you. This is a large facility, and modern art really runs the gamut from some of the more expected paintings (like those listed above) to other works that may seem confusing or hold little interest for children. We advise sticking to what you think you will like, and going in with a plan of attack.

Parents Note: Modern art has a reputation for daring, and for pushing boundaries. We recommend sticking to the paintings and more popular selections above if visiting with young children. Some of the video and photography exhibits may present material unsuitable for young children, though the museum does a good job of designating such areas.

Address: 11 W 53rd St, New York, NY 10019

Phone: (212) 708-9400

Hours: Saturday - Wednesday, 10:30 AM - 5:30 PM. Thursday & Friday, 10:30 AM - 8 PM.

Website: www.moma.org/

Approximate Cost: Adults, $25. Students, $14. Children (16 and Under), FREE. You can purchase tickets online in advance.

Approximate Length: For visits with children, we advise spending **1-2 hours** here to keep them engaged.

Chinatown

Why We Omitted It: Our main itinerary swings through SoHo and a couple other neighborhoods that have many different things to offer, in an effort to provide "something for everyone." If you know that this is something that appeals for you, and want to experience the authentic flair, then we say this is a great neighborhood to explore.

Where it Goes: Ideally on Day 5 in lower Manhattan, though easy subway access means you could tag it onto the end of Day 1 or 7 as well.

Bordered by the Lower East Side to the east, Little Italy to the north, Civic Center to the south, and Tribeca to the west - this neighborhood is in the heart of a thriving and exciting part of the city. Chinatown contributes greatly to this atmosphere with a fascinating glimpse at another culture. Featuring the largest enclave of Chinese people in the entire Western Hemisphere, Chinatown NYC has served as the inspiration for numerous similar neighborhoods throughout the country and the world.

The history of Chinatown is a fascinating look at the immigrant experience in New York City. Purported as the first Chinese immigrant to settle here, a man named Ah Ken found fortune as a cigar merchant. Later, Ken opened a boarding house on Mott Street that would house other immigrants from China and open the doors to a booming Chinese population here, during the period from 1840 to the 1860's. Persecution in other parts of the west (including the Chinese Exclusion Act of 1882) led to a massive influx of Chinese nationals to New York in the 1870's. Chinatown began with businesses designed to serve the rest of the city, followed by small Chinese groceries and herbal shops to support the burgeoning Chinese population.

As the relatively small community continued to grow, it became a center of immigration, culture, and recreation for the Chinese community in New York City. It was self-segregated from the rest of New York, not by discrimination from outsiders, but out of economic realities. Eventually, limited opportunities for growth experienced by many merchants led to the encouragement of tourism. Difficulty breaking into the "mainstream" and getting work outside of Chinatown led locals to the notion of "why not bring the city to us?"

In many ways, Chinatown also mirrors the experiences of many other immigrant societies in New York City, including the early Irish, Italian, and Jewish New Yorkers. While sites like Ellis Island help tell the tale of individuals looking for their place upon entering America, Chinatown tells the story of a community, one that had trouble finding opportunities at first, but whose indomitable spirit carved a unique version of the American dream out of the downtown area.

Travel Tip: If you are interested in learning more about the Chinese and immigrant story in New York City, visit the Museum of Chinese in America (MOCA) at 215 Centre Street.

Exploring Chinatown as a family is an experience to share. Grab a meal at a great restaurant - part of the fun is just wandering and seeing what looks good.

There is also a lot of fun to be had in walking the streets and browsing the shops, or seeing what is being sold on the streets. No matter how well versed you may be in exotic ingredients and goods, you are all but guaranteed to spot something along the way that makes you ask, "what *is* that thing?!" Children will delight at the sight of live fish, small animals, and all manner of exotic goods you would be hard pressed to find elsewhere.

Walking the streets of Chinatown is an opportunity to explore another culture and to feel transported to another world while travelling a few small blocks. Take in the atmosphere and indulge in whatever forms of local culture appeal to you. You may want to look at a map online before your visit, in order to plan a route, or you may just want to show up and see where the experience takes you.

Address: Canal Street to Worth/Bayard Streets, Between Broadway and Essex

Hours: Vary by establishment, though families may get more out of it in the late morning/midday.

Website: www.explorechinatown.com/

Approximate Cost: Free to explore, food varies greatly by establishment.

Approximate Length: How long you spend here depends on what you want to do, but an **hour to an hour and a half** will give you enough time to walk and explore, as well as grab a quick meal.

Lower East Side Tenement Museum

Why We Omitted It: Because the museum can only be seen on a guided tour, and time and availability of these tours vary, we chose to include activities with more flexibility in the main itinerary. The subject matter here is fascinating, and if you are willing to lock into a time, this museum is a great learning experience.

Where it Goes: Makes most sense on Day 5 in lower Manhattan.

The building at 97 Orchard Street served as a tenement from 1863 to 1935. The 5 story, multi-occupancy, brick building is estimated to have been the home for some 7,000 people in those 72 years. These residents represent some 20 different nationalities, and are a powerful example of the immigrant experience in New York City.

The building evolved greatly over the years that it served as low-income housing. In its earliest years, it contained 22 apartment units and a basement saloon. Over time, basement and street level spaces were converted to retail use, and modern conveniences including gas heat, electricity, and indoor plumbing were slowly added. Eventually apartments were boarded up and remained empty for years while the retail space remained open. The unique story of the building created a wonderfully preserved history of 19th and 20th century living conditions - the different modifications to various areas representing the evolution of what was considered acceptable for housing over the years.

These circumstances created an ideal setting for a museum to depict and exhibit the immigrant experience in New York City, as well as the history of housing and public standards. Inside, the exhibits include restored apartments representing the stories and lives of specific immigrants who resided at 97 Orchard Street between 1869 and 1935. Actors help bring the stories to life as their costumed interpretations allow you to "meet the residents" and further expand your view of the time. At the core of the museum's mission is to promote tolerance and historical perspective on the immigrant experience.

The ONLY way to experience the museum is on a guided tour. You cannot wander on your own. This allows the museum to present a more richly developed experience, as you tour apartments and businesses, meet the "residents", and walk the neighborhood in order to see how the area and its culture both shaped and were shaped by its immigrant residents.

Travel Tip: It is <u>strongly</u> suggested that you purchase tickets online in advance. Tickets and tours open up **one month** before the date.

Just Some of the Guided Tour Options Include:

- **Shop Life** - Learn about family-run stores and 100 years of tales that depict families searching for the

American dream *(Ground floor - 90 minutes - Recommended Ages 12+)*.
- **Sweatshop Workers** (see also, **Sweatshop Workers: Tour and Discussion**) - Go back to a time when the Lower East Side was the most densely populated place in the world, and learn how immigrants balanced busy lives of work and family *(3rd Floor - 1 Hour - Recommended Ages 8+)*.
- **Hard Times** (see also, **Hard Times: Tour and Discussion**) - Learn how the Great Depression affected immigrants of various backgrounds, who were among New York City's poorest citizens *(2nd Floor - 1 Hour - Recommended Ages 8+)*.
- **Irish Outsiders** - Learn how one particular family of Irish immigrants coped with being outsiders and the death of a child, through an exploration of their home and music *(4th Floor - 1 Hour - Recommended Ages 12+)*.
- **Exploring 97 Orchard** - This behind the scenes tour shows how urban archaeologists have interpreted the various layers of paint, wallpaper, and construction to deduce the story of the building and its residents *(Only Offered on Thursdays - 1st, 2nd, & 4th Floors - 90 Minutes - Recommended Ages 12+)*.

Meet The Residents Opportunities:
- **Victoria Confino** - *NOTE: This is the ONLY option for those with children under 6.* This tour introduces you to the 14 year old daughter of a Greek Sephardic family. Play the role of new immigrants, asking Victoria questions about how best to adapt to life in the tenement for an interactive experience *(1st Floor - 1 Hour - Recommended Ages 5+)*.
- **Tenement Inspectors** and **Live! At the Tenement** - Only offered on select dates, these interactive extravaganzas feature multiple interpreters, allowing you to get the stories of landlords and tenants as they interact, as well as the intersections in the residents' daily lives.

Outdoor Tours:

- **Buildings on the Lower East Side** - Learn about the architects, artists, and everyday people who shaped the neighborhood as you explore on foot and admire real life examples *(2 Hours - Recommended Ages 8+)*.
- **Storefront Stories** - Learn about small business ownership, haggling, and other realities as you compare the experiences of immigrant entrepreneurs in the past and present *(75 Minutes - Recommended Ages 8+)*.
- **Outside The Home** - Learn about various facets of immigrant life on this guided walk. From banks and schools to labor unions, learn about the "supporting cast" of neighborhood institutions on the Lower East Side *(90 Minutes - Recommended Ages 8+)*.
- **Then & Now** - This tour centers on the residents of the neighborhood, and how they have helped to shape the area and improve it over the years, in the face of social and political revolution *(2 Hours - Recommended Ages 8+)*.

Prior to the rapid gentrification of the late 20th century, the Lower East Side represented an important working class and immigrant enclave within Manhattan, as it launched so many lives and careers. This melting pot of culture long stood as a launching point for the American dream, and thus serves as a perfect representation of what many of us think of when we contemplate the history of New York City. The Lower East Side Tenement Museum offers a unique and immersive opportunity to explore this history as a family, through interactive exhibits that combine the building, the residents, and the neighborhood into one rich story.

Choose whatever tour best suits your family, and enjoy the unique means to explore history. The fact that the museum promotes tolerance and an exploration of shared values is an added bonus. Your family will also enjoy the opportunity to grow closer as you explore the stories of not-so-different families from the past, learning about the sacrifice and hard work that went into building a better life against the odds. This is one New York City landmark that combines history, culture, and values into one excellent experience.

Address: 97 Orchard St, New York, NY 10002

Phone: (877) 975-3786

Hours: Tour times vary by date and tour chosen. See their online calendar for specific hours.

Website: www.tenement.org/

Approximate Cost: Adults, $25. Students, $20. Tours involving food cost $45 for Adults and $40 for Students. Order tickets online, up to one month in advance.

Please Note: Infants, toddlers, and all **children under 6 years old are NOT allowed** on the building tours, with the exception of the "Meet Victoria Confino" tour.

Approximate Length: Expect to spend **1-2 hours** here for your in-building tour (each tour has an approximate time). This stop may be even longer if you wish to wander the neighborhood.

Explore Rockefeller Center

Why We Omitted It: This location lies somewhat between the planned activities of our midtown days and the one spent downtown. This means it can easily be added to any of them, though we felt it was a bit out of the way of our planned routes.

Where it Goes: Any of days 1, 5 or 7.

This quintessential New York experience is world famous and instantly recognizable. The complex of 19 commercial buildings, including offices, upscale shopping and dining, as well as a beautiful open plaza - was originally commissioned by the Rockefeller family. Originally, John D. Rockefeller, Jr. leased the land from Columbia University, with plans to build an opera house on the site. The market crash of 1929 changed those plans, and Rockefeller pushed on with commercial development, funded entirely out of pocket.

Grab a bite in one of many great restaurants and do a little souvenir shopping. There are a variety of fun stores for kids featuring games and toys, as well as a selection of upscale and mid-range boutiques for adults. Pop in for the unique fun of the NBC Experience Store and you might just catch a glimpse of someone famous. Also be sure to check out the current special offers and sales for "Rock Center."

Over the years a lot of history took place here, including the famous "Room 3603" which served as the principal operations center for Allied intelligence during World War II, as well as the office of the forerunner to the Central Intelligence Agency.

Also part of Rockefeller Center is the famous Radio City Music Hall, located at 1260 Avenue of the Americas. This internationally recognized 6,000 seat venue is home to a number of concerts and shows every year, a favorite tourist destination, and the site of the annual Radio City Christmas Spectacular. See their calendar for a chance to book a show during your stay.

Your family may also enjoy the fantastic views from the highest levels of 30 Rockefeller Plaza, on the "Top of the Rock" tour. If you plan on visiting the Empire State Building as part of our main itinerary it may be a bit redundant (in our view, the informational displays and tour are quite different) but if you choose to forgo that stop, this is another terrific option.

During the late fall and winter, there are some special opportunities here as well. Starting sometime in November, there is the chance to see New York City's most famous Christmas tree, as the annual bastion of holiday cheer is installed in the plaza. There is also the chance to skate the famous ice in front of "30 Rock," the home of famous NBC television shows and impressive Art Deco architecture.

Skating is on a first come, first serve basis and it does get crowded. If you want to ensure a spot, for a little extra you can reserve ice time through either the VIP Skate or First Skate packages. "First Skate" allows you in at 7 AM, before the ice is open to the public and includes a hot beverage to get your day going. For another ice skating opportunity and great alternative should you skip Rockefeller Plaza, see Trump Rink in Central Park (the next alternate stop).

Address: 45 Rockefeller Plaza New York, NY 10111 (5th Avenue between 49th and 50th Streets)

Phone: (212) 332-6868

Hours: Vary by location, ice skating is seasonal (opens in October, runs through the winter).

Website: www.rockefellercenter.com/

Approximate Cost: Food and activities vary by location, free to browse.

Approximate Length: We recommend spending **1-2 hours** here, depending on how much browsing and shopping you want to do, as well as whether or not you take a meal here.

LATE FALL/WINTER - Ice Skating at Trump Rink

Why We Omitted It: This is a great activity that we highly recommend, but the outdoor ice skating is seasonal so it didn't make sense to put it in the main itinerary for families travelling other times of the year.

Where it Goes: Any of days 1, 5 or 7 - though the Central Park location makes most sense on the first day, followed by the last.

PLEASE NOTE: The skating begins sometime in early October of each year and continues through the winter. Check their website for exact dates.

Trump Rink (sometimes known as Wollman Rink) brings the joy of ice skating right to the heart of Central Park. Enjoy this quintessential fall and winter activity in an open air environment while still enjoying views of some of the city's most spectacular buildings.

Ice skating in New York City can be an especially rewarding activity for families during a vacation. It gives you a chance to take a break from the sightseeing and educational opportunities - to cut loose and blow off some steam. Considering the rink is also a favorite of native New Yorkers, it is also a nice chance to rub elbows with locals, and enjoy something everyone can get behind, together.

While there are locations spread throughout the 5 boroughs that offer outdoor skating, enjoying a skate in Central Park is a terrific experience. This is our favorite spot to lace up some skates and enjoy the chilly winter air, followed by a warm cup of cocoa as you share some laughs and enjoy the change of pace.

VIP packages are available online for an additional fee. These allow you to cut the line as well as receive some nice benefits like warm drinks, snacks, and a heated rest area.

Spring/Summer Tip: In the warmer months, Trump Rink becomes "Victorian Gardens" - a summer amusement park facility. See the next alternate stop for details.

Address: 59th St, New York, NY 10023

Phone: (212) 439-6900

Hours: Monday/Tuesday 10 AM - 2:30 PM

Wednesday/Thursday 10 AM - 10 PM

Friday/Saturday 10 AM - 11 PM

Sunday 10 AM - 9 PM

Website: www.trumprink.com/

Approximate Cost: Monday - Thursday: Adults $11.25, Children (11 and under) $6, Seniors $5. Friday - Sunday (and Holidays): Adults $18, Children $6, Seniors $9. Skate Rentals $8, Locker Rentals $5 (plus refundable $6 deposit).

Approximate Length: Depending on how much you like to skate, an **hour** or so will likely be enough before you are ready to come out of the cold.

SPRING/SUMMER - Amusement Park at Victorian Gardens

Why We Omitted It: This is another seasonal activity that is a lot of fun, but limited availability kept it off the list for the main itinerary.

Where it Goes: Any of days 1, 5 or 7 - though the Central Park location makes most sense on the first day, followed by the last.

In the spring and summer, Trump Rink (sometimes known as Wollman Rink) hangs up its ice skates and opens the doors to outdoor amusement park fun.

Known as "Victorian Gardens" in the warmer months, this summer amusement park facility comes complete with rides, entertainment, and more. Enjoy traditional carnival fare as you play games of chance, or take a ride on the Kite Flyer, RainboWheel, or Magic Bike. There are even bumper boats on the water, for a real slice of something different in the heart of Central Park.

The shows each weekend are geared towards families, offering a mix of comedy, magic, and silly antics to delight and amuse children. Some shows are interactive, and all are geared towards breaking up a hot summer day with some good old fashioned family fun.

Address: 59th St, New York, NY 10023

Phone: (212) 982-2229

Email: info@victoriangardensnyc.com

Hours: The park opens between 10 and 11 AM, and closes between 7 and 9 PM (see calendar for exact times).

Website: www.victoriangardensnyc.com/

Approximate Cost: Weekdays $8 Admission, $15 for unlimited rides wristband. Weekends $9 admission, $17 for unlimited rides wristband. Ride tickets can also be purchased for $1 each, 4 tickets per ride. **NOTE:** wristbands do not include games.

Approximate Length: We recommend an **hour or two** here to enjoy a few rides and possibly some food.

Take in a Broadway Show

Why We Omitted It: For the purpose of keeping this book timeless, it is difficult to recommend a particular show seeing as they open and close all the time. We also recognize that the theater isn't for everyone, though we do recommend pushing your comfort zone a little to share this experience with your family.

Where it Goes: Great way to end any of the days if you can cut off touring early enough, easiest on a day already in Manhattan, including days 1, 5 and 7.

A great Broadway experience is the kind of memory that can last a lifetime for a family. You can create a great bonding moment as you share in the splendor and tradition of the stage, while enjoying the heart of New York City. Whether you live in the area, or are looking to make a trip to fabulous New York - with all it has to offer children, teens, and parents - we highly recommend a stop on the "Great White Way." Experience the unique segment of culture and excitement that collide when the lights go down in a Broadway Theater.

Spanning the area between 40th and 54th Streets, between 8th Avenue and 6th, you'll find the world of arts and entertainment known as the theatre district. Here, you will find some of the best live performance of the world, in a location that unites New Yorkers and tourists in their pursuit of a great time.

Travel Tip: Many restaurants in this area will offer special seatings that mind opening times for shows, and get you in and out quickly rather than sit through a show waiting to eat afterwards.

At any given time there are somewhere in the neighborhood of 30-40 shows operating in the area, ranging from musical extravaganzas (most of them) to quieter dramas. The shows also run the gamut from adult content to family friendly, though there are always a number of great options to take the kids to. An exposure to theatre for young children is an invaluable experience, and a quintessential New York City memory to share together.

Travel Tip: While Broadway tickets are notoriously expensive, families looking for money can visit the TKTS booth (sponsored by the Theatre Development Fund) for day-of tickets that are often considerably cheaper as shows try to sell off and fill empty seats. You might also check out the ticket deals on www.GoldStar.com.

Hours for TKTS Booths:

For evening performances:

Monday, Wednesday, Thursday, Friday, Saturday: 3 PM - 8PM. Tuesday: 2 PM - 8 PM. Sunday: 3 PM - 7PM.

For matinee performances:

Wednesday and Saturday: 10 AM - 2 PM.

Sunday: 11AM - 3 PM.

Visit Broadway.org for a full listing of current shows, and determine what it is that appeals most to your family. You can also call Tele-charge (212-239-6200 or 800-432-7250) or Ticketmaster (212-307-4100 or 800-755-4000) for listings and to purchase tickets; though note that a service charge may apply.

Travel Tip: Broadway.org also offers an app for Android or for iOS, to let you browse on the fly, as well as build up excitement for the experience.

As of the time of this publication, the show we recommend for families is Finding Neverland. Billed as "The Story of How Peter Became Pan", Finding Neverland: The Musical brings a childhood classic to the stage in an exciting and vibrant new performance.

Read our RealFamilyTrips.com full spotlight on the show at:

http://realfamilytrips.com/spotlight-on-finding-neverland-and-family-fun-on-broadway-in-nyc/

The High Bridge (and Highbridge Park)

Why We Omitted It: The grand reopening of this bridge only barely preceded the printing of this book. It missed the cut for our main itinerary only because of this time factor, so we made sure to include it in the alternate activities.

Where it Goes: Any Manhattan Day (1, 5, or 7), though makes most sense on Day 1 or 7. Alternately, you could end your Bronx day (Day 2) here and use this as a way to cross back into Manhattan.

Closed for nearly 40 years, as of June 9, 2015 New York City's oldest standing bridge is back in business. Now the hottest "new" pedestrian walkway and sightseeing opportunity in all of New York, this bridge that connects northern Manhattan with the Bronx is giving New Yorkers and tourists alike a lot to talk about.

With a structure that evokes a Roman aqueduct, the High Bridge opened in 1848. It was built as part of the Croton Aqueduct, a system constructed to deliver water from the New York State river of the same name. The original stone arch bridge helped deliver water to the early inhabitants of a burgeoning city, and helped fuel the rapid expansion of Manhattan. The bridge also helped to transform the area that surrounded it, still rural at the time of its construction, into an area for recreation and sport. The regal stone arches served as a perfect backdrop for regattas and other aquatic events. Nearby land used for carriage races and parades resulted in a roadway that would evolve to become the Harlem River Drive.

After doing much to shape New York City as a whole, and the area of Washington Heights (around 174th Street) that surrounds the Manhattan end of the bridge, it fell on tough times. A 1928 renovation replaced the stone archways with steel ones, to allow for better water traffic underneath. Modern advancements saw the end of the bridge as a water supply in 1948, with responsibility for the bridge transferring to the New York City Parks Department in 1955. The bridge was closed in the 1970's. Now, some 40 years and 61.8 million dollars later, this fixture of the New York City skyline has been reimagined.

The bridge that once brought water has been reinvented as a way to provide easy pedestrian passage between The Bronx and Manhattan, as well as great panoramic views of the Harlem River. New Yorkers and tourists are both getting excited about the reopening of this historical bridge, with unique views that have been inaccessible for years. Whether you take advantage of it as a way to cross from one borough to another, or simply come to enjoy the scenery, this is a fantastic way to dive into New York City history in a very different way.

You may also choose to expand this stop by either beginning, or ending, with a visit to adjoining Highbridge Park, and enjoy the park in much the same way New Yorkers of old did. Highlights of the park include the Adventure Playground, as well as Coogan's Bluff. The bluff was the onetime home of the Polo Grounds, the playing field for the former New York Giants baseball team. The park also features bicycling paths, a recreation center, and plenty of green space for sports and relaxation.

Address: To enter the High Bridge from the **Manhattan side**, enter Highbridge Park at 172nd Street and Amsterdam Avenue and walk east to the High Bridge Water Tower Terrace staircase (for stroller/wheelchair access, use the ramp located at 167th Street and Edgecombe Avenue). From the **Bronx side**, enter at University Avenue and 170th Street in Highbridge, Bronx.

Phone: (212) 408-0100

Hours: Park/Bridge open daily from 7 AM - 8 PM in the summer. There may still be occasional closures for construction. To check for availability, and for hours in other seasons, see their website.

Website: www.nycgovparks.org/parks/highbridge-park

Approximate Cost: FREE of charge.

Approximate Length: We recommend about a **half hour to an hour** here.

The Bronx

Hall of Fame for Great Americans

Why We Omitted It: This quaint location doesn't demand a lot of time, but with big stops like the New York Botanical Garden and Bronx Zoo - we chose to allow more time in the main itinerary to really soak in those experiences. If you want or are willing to do either of those stops a little more quickly (or strike any of the stops altogether), this is a great option.

Where it Goes: Day 2.

The Hall of Fame of Great Americans, located on the campus of Bronx Community College, is a landmark, an educational opportunity, and a slice of real Bronx living - all rolled into one. Founded in 1900 by Dr. Henry Mitchell MacCracken, Chancellor of New York University from 1891 to 1910, it was originally planned for NYU's campus. The goal then was the same as it was now - to honor prominent Americans who have had a significant impact on the nation's history.

This original "hall of fame" is the one that gave birth to the many specialized institutions across the nation (and the world) that honor the greats of certain fields. Some of the notables honored here include Alexander Graham Bell, Eli Whitney, and George Westinghouse. Occupations and roles of the famous honorees include inventors, explorers, teachers, authors, architects, scientists, statesmen, artists, musicians, actors, and judges. The hall includes 102 niches for sculptures.

All honorees are depicted with bronze busts, created by prominent American sculptors. Bronze tablets recessed in the wall beneath the busts bear inscriptions of significant statements made by the men and women featured in the hall. Among the artists represented with sculptures in the hall are Daniel Chester French (designer of the Lincoln Memorial) and James Earl Fraser (whose work includes the figures of "Justice" and "Law" for the U.S. Supreme Court).

Since 1900, 102 individuals have been approved by the committee to select prominent Americans, while 98 of the honorees are currently depicted with statues and plaques.

The hall is adorned by a semicircular Neo-Classical arc with wings at either end, framing a stunning 630-foot open-air colonnade designed by famed architect Stanford White. The entire facility offers a panoramic view across the Harlem River to the Cloisters in Fort Tryon Park, and beyond to the Palisades and New Jersey.

PLEASE NOTE: Since this site is located on an active college campus, a **Photo ID is required** to visit, for security purposes.

A visit here with family is great for several reasons. First, the inexpensive option allows you to enjoy the opportunity for art and education without breaking the bank. Second, it is located in a terrific setting - you will see turn of the century architecture, in addition to the regal busts that adorn the sweeping colonnade. Finally, the site offers a chance to dive into history and educate children - about the famous names and faces, as well as the intellectual power and ingenuity of their achievements. To visit the hall is to help inspire the next generation of great Americans.

Address: 2155 University Ave, Bronx, NY 10453

Phone: (718) 289-5170

Email: remo.cosentino@bcc.cuny.edu or therese.lemelle@bcc.cuny.edu (email before going if you want a group tour - 2 weeks advance notice is recommended)

Hours: Weekdays, 9 AM - 5 PM. Weekends, 10 AM - 4 PM.

Website: www.bcc.cuny.edu/halloffame/

Approximate Cost: FREE to do a self-guided tour, although a $2 donation per visitor is appreciated. Group tours cost $25 for up to 15 people.

Approximate Length: We recommend about **an hour** here, less if you just want to admire the structure and see a couple of statues.

Bartow-Pell Mansion Museum and Carriage House

Why We Omitted It: While a great stop for families, limited days and hours of operation made it hard to recommend this stop for the main itinerary. If the Bronx day of your trip happens to coincide with the scheduled days it is open, consider adding it or swapping it in during the afternoon.

Where it Goes: Day 2.

Tucked away in the quiet corner of Pelham Bay, The Bronx, this grand manor and its grounds provide an incredible window to the past. Built between 1836 and 1842, this mansion and its adjoining gardens and grounds are representative of the days when Pelham Park was considered "country living" - and giant estates owned by the wealthiest New Yorkers defined the area.

The mansion and its grounds as they stand today are part of a nearly 9,000-acre tract purchased from the Siwanoy Indians by Thomas Pell, an English doctor from Connecticut. Following the Revolutionary War, the estate was reduced to about 200 acres. Acquired in 1836 by Robert Bartow, the existing Grecian style stone mansion with Greek Revival interiors was built and occupied by the Bartow family beginning in 1842. While the similar mansions of the surrounding area gave way and were sold off for development and other ventures, this home remained - opened to the public as a museum in 1946.

Now the only grand country house still in existence on Pelham Bay, this site provides an important link to the social and architectural history of New York. See how the estate looks, and compare it to the now developed surrounding area. This opportunity to juxtapose the past and the present demonstrates how New York City has changed, and allows your family an opportunity to step back from the urbanized surroundings to a simpler time.

Visitors are welcome to take a guided tour of the mansion and view the impressive collection of mid-19th century furnishings and fine and decorative arts; group Tours are available by appointment only. Alternately (or if visiting on a weekday that does not offer tours/mansion access), you can choose to walk around the grounds and the terraced garden behind the house.

Address: 895 Shore Rd, Bronx, NY 10464

Phone: (718) 885-1461

Hours: Mansion - Wednesday, Saturday and Sunday: 12 PM - 4 PM. Closed Monday, Tuesday, Thursday and Friday. Gardens and Grounds - Open Daily from 8:30 AM - Dusk.

Website: www.bartowpellmansionmuseum.org/

Approximate Cost: Mansion - $5 for adults, $3 for Students, FREE for Children under 6. Gardens are FREE to all.

Approximate Length: We recommend **1-2 hours** here.

The Van Cortlandt House Museum

Why We Omitted It: This great historic house really is an interesting visit - however in a borough that has The Bronx Zoo and The New York Botanical Garden, it is less universally appealing than some other options. If your kids are older and may want to skip the zoo or another stop, this is a terrific substitution.

Where it Goes: Day 2.

This Georgian style home (also known as the Frederick Van Cortlandt House) is the single oldest building in the entire borough of The Bronx. Built in 1748 for Frederick's family, the house has seen a lot of history. It was used by Comte de Rochambeau, The Marquis de Lafayette, and George Washington (who stayed here at least twice during the Revolutionary War). It was also the former location of a grain plantation and grist mill, operated by the Van Cortlandt family.

In 1889, after 140 years of Van Cortlandt occupancy, the house was sold to the City of New York for use as a public park, and operated as a historic house museum ever since 1897. This was the first home in New York to be converted to a museum in this manner, and only the fourth in the United States. Thus, besides the history of the house itself, this museum marks an important milestone in historical preservation and education for the city and the country.

Travel Tip: According to the museum itself "It is always a good idea for you to call Van Cortlandt House before your visit. The museum occasionally has to close due to the weather, fallen tree branches, old-house problems, film shoots, and restoration projects. There are also times when we are required to close due to conditions in the park outside our fence."

Inside you will find an impressive collection of heirlooms donated by the Van Cortlandt family. There are period furnishings and beautiful works of art, as well as artifacts that mark everyday life from the nearly century and a half the home was occupied. The house shares the story of one early New York family, their rise to prominence, and their role in shaping the future of the city. Additionally, you will learn about the many famous and influential people who visited the home, and the important things that happened here. This is a place where ordinary New Yorkers, great historical figures - as well as ordinary New Yorkers who *became* great historical figures - come together.

Travel Tip: Wednesdays are FREE admission days. You are still welcome to donate, but can get general admission at no charge.

You can choose to wander on your own, or take a group tour that lasts about an hour, led by Michael Grillo, the Van Cortlandt House Museum Educator. Contact him by email two weeks in advance to arrange a tour. Whether you take the group tour or explore on your own, themes will include the Revolutionary War, life in Little Yonkers, and the highlights of the museum's collection. To take yourselves around, it is recommended that you download the self-guided tour booklet for free from the museum's website.

Address: 6036 Broadway, Van Cortlandt Park, Bronx, NY 10471

Phone: (718) 543-3344

Email: michael.grillo@vchm.org (contact for group tours)

Hours: Tuesday - Friday, 10 AM - 3 PM. Saturday and Sunday, 11 AM - 4 PM. Closed Mondays.

Website: www.vchm.org/

Approximate Cost: General Admission - Adults, $5. Students, $3. Children under 12 are FREE. Group tours are an additional $5 for adults, $3 for children.

Approximate Length: We recommend about **1 hour** here.

Brooklyn

Brooklyn Botanic Garden

Why We Omitted It: We chose to include the New York Botanical Garden in The Bronx, as well as Snug Harbor in Staten Island, both of which have similar offerings to this stop. If you choose to skip either or both, or simply want to take in as much nature as you can - this is a great addition/substitution.

Where it Goes: Day 3.

Founded in 1910, this facility within the Prospect Park section of Brooklyn is a 52 acre garden and park area with a special focus on education. Particularly family friendly and possessing a large number of educational programs for children, the BBG - as some call it - offers an escape from the busier parts of the city and a wealth of variety in plant life. With several smaller, distinct gardens within the larger facility, you and your children can explore a world of plants and cross oceans without ever leaving Brooklyn.

Travel Tip: The annual Cherry Blossom Festival is a family favorite. Every year in April, the garden celebrates the blooming of the stunning trees with food, costumes, and fun that make the garden a must-visit when travelling in April. The month-long festival of *Hanami*, a Japanese tradition, is held at the Cherry Esplanade, ending with a weekend celebration called *Sakura Matsuri*.

While the Garden's website makes it easy to check what is in bloom at a given time, as well as what events and activities are on the calendar, there are a number of specialty gardens and areas that make this facility truly unique - and are worth popping by any time you are in the area:

- **Cherry Trees:** the garden has over 200 specimens representing 42 varieties of the Asian cherry tree. They were originally planted in the 1920's - a gift from the Japanese government following World War I. The different species bloom at slightly different times, but generally begin in late March or early April and bloom through mid-May. Keep an eye online with the cherry blossom tracker.
- **Japanese Hill-and-Pond Garden:** This was the first Japanese garden created within an American public garden space. Opened in 1915 and designed by Japanese landscape designer Takeo Shiota, the garden blends hills, ponds, and open areas for a variety of authentic features and is a beautiful sight to behold. You may also enjoy the traditional architectural elements which include wooden bridges, a torii (gateway), stone lanterns, and a Shinto shrine.
- **Shakespeare Garden:** This garden opened in 1925 and was donated/conceived by Henry Clay Folger, founder of the Folger Shakespeare Library in Washington, D.C. It features an English cottage style, and over 80 varieties of plants and flowers mentioned in the poems and plays of William Shakespeare. Older children beginning to study Shakespeare in school will enjoy the setting, as well as the way plants are interwoven with quotes, Shakespearean names, and fun facts related to the great author.

- **The Children's Garden:** Opened in 1915, this is the oldest continually operated children's garden (within a botanic garden) in the entire world. Each year, hundreds of children register for small plots on which they are able to grow their own plants for food, fun, and education. Your children will enjoy the opportunity to see what some of their contemporaries have done, as well as the opportunity to learn about community gardening practices in a location that has served as a model for many other such programs around the world.
- You will also find the **Cranford Rose Garden**, **The Native Flora Garden** (dedicated to the native flora of the New York Metropolitan area), the **Alice Recknagel Ireys Fragrance Garden** (featuring fragrant plants you are encouraged to touch, and designed for the visually impaired), the **Steinhardt Conservatory** (for indoor plants, including the Bonsai Museum) and the **Plant Family Collection** (which arranges plants by family to show genetic relationships and evolutionary progression).

All this only begins to scratch the surface of what is available at the Brooklyn Botanical Garden. From facilities dating back to the turn of the 20th century, to brand new offerings like the Discovery Garden - this facility is constantly reinventing itself and giving families new and exciting reasons to visit. See some beautiful plant life, learn information about nature you can use when you get home, and meet kids on their level as you all participate in Family Activities that you can enjoy together.

Address: 990 Washington Ave, Brooklyn, NY 11225

Phone: (718) 623-7200

Email: visitorservices@bbg.org

Hours: Tuesday - Saturday, 8 AM - 6 PM. Saturday and Sunday, 10 AM - 6 PM. Closed Mondays.

Website: www.bbg.org/

Approximate Cost: Adults, $12. Students, $6. Children under 12 are FREE.

Approximate Length: We recommend about **2 hours** here, unless there is a special event going on that you would like to participate in.

New York Transit Museum

Why We Omitted It: This stop is a little out of the way of our main itinerary for Brooklyn, so we chose to omit it in order to keep the day more linear.

Where it Goes: Day 3.

Please Note: This is for the main facility of the Transit Museum, located in Brooklyn. There is also an annex and store in Grand Central Station (Located just off the main concourse in the Shuttle Passage, adjacent to the Station Master's Office).

With millions of citizens, a spread of five boroughs separated by land and water, and a city that grew organically from many plans as opposed to one unified vision; the challenge of getting citizens from one place to another efficiently has always been one of the great challenges for New York City. Hailed as having one of the most complex, accessible, and far reaching public transit systems in the world, the Metropolitan Transportation Authority (and its predecessors) have handled the seemingly impossible task of moving New Yorkers from point A to point B through some of the greatest ingenuity around.

The Transit Museum is the largest facility devoted to urban public transportation history in the United States. Enjoy exhibitions, tours, educational programs, and workshops that allow you and your family to go inside the workings of New York City's buses, subways, light rail, and other forms of public transit. More than just depicting the logistics of getting around, this museum looks at the cultural, social, and technological history of urban transportation. Learn how New York City developed its means of getting around, and what it taught the world, as you explore one of the most influential factors of urban life which is too often taken for granted.

The museum is housed in a historic 1936 IND subway station in Downtown Brooklyn. Among the permanent exhibits you and your children will find:

- **Steel, Stone & Backbone: Building New York's Subways 1900-1925** - learn the story of how the 100 year-old subway system was made, through artifacts, videos and photos from the course of the construction. Put faces to the ubiquitous rail system as you see the men and women who designed, built, and operated the subway from its earliest days.
- **On the Streets: New York's Trolleys and Buses** - is a fun, interactive exhibit that is perfect for children. Participate in a simulated intersection complete with traffic lights, signs, parking meters, fire hydrants, and more. Board refurbished antique buses and trolleys, and get involved in experiencing the roots of modern transit.
- **Fare Collection** - teaches about the history of paying your way, with examples of past technology used to collect fares for public transit. Many of the examples allow you to interact with them and "pay" for a ride, allowing children to experience the ways of the past and step inside history.
- See a full list of New Exhibits and Long-term Exhibits on their website.

You will also want to take a look at their Children's and Family Programs. This facility provides unique insight into an important part of the New York City experience, lending context to the rest of your visit, as you teach your children how the things we use every day came to be.

Address: Boerum Place & Schermerhorn Street, Brooklyn, NY 11201

Phone: (718) 694-1600

Hours: Tuesday - Friday, 10 AM - 4 PM. Saturday and Sunday, 11 AM - 5 PM. Closed Mondays.

Website: http://web.mta.info/mta/museum/

Approximate Cost: Adults, $7. Children (2-17), $5.

Approximate Length: We recommend visiting for about **an hour** here.

Brooklyn Academy of Music (See a Show)

Why We Omitted It: The main attraction here is to see a show or other performance, which involves a lot of variables. Our main itinerary works under most conditions, but if you want to find a show that looks good for you and your kids, and wind up here at the end of the day, it can be a great way to take in the arts.

Where it Goes: Day 3, probably best for end of day.

Brooklyn Academy of Music, affectionately known as "BAM," is the oldest continually operated performing arts space in the country, tracing its roots back to 1859. Here you will find a wide array of performance and visual arts - including theatre, film, dance, and some food to round out the experience. They have a number of family friendly and kid-oriented shows on at a given time, and taking in a performance here can be a real treat.

While it may be known for its progressive and avant garde performance in artistic circles, it also has a reputation for variety. With three main performance spaces, you'll want to take a look at what is happening at each:

- **Peter Jay Sharp Building** - includes the BAM Howard Gilman Opera House, BAM Rose Cinemas, BAMcafé, and Hillman Attic Studio.
- **BAM Harvey Theater**
- **BAM Fisher** - includes the Fishman Space, BAM Fisher Hillman Studio, BAM Fisher Rooftop Terrace, and the Leavitt Workshop.

You and your family will be in good company at this theater space with a rich history. First Lady Mary Todd Lincoln attended the first ever performance here, the opera Il Giuramento. Notable performances over the years include readings from Mark Twain, the American debut of The Royal Shakespeare Company, and modern era appearances by the likes of Cate Blanchett, Paul Simon, and Robert Redford.

See the visitor's page on their website to browse the current offerings. You can look by venue, or go straight to their kid's section to find family friendly fare.

Address: 30 Lafayette Ave, Brooklyn, NY 11217

Phone: (718) 636-4100

Hours: Varies by what you want to see.

Website: www.bam.org/

Approximate Cost: Varies by what you want to see.

Approximate Length: Varies, your best bet is to end the day here with a show, stay until it is over and wind your way back to wherever you are staying.

Staten Island

Jacques Marchais Museum of Tibetan Art

Why We Omitted It: The limited days and hours for this museum made it difficult to recommend for our main itinerary out of concern for families having to plan their entire trip around it. If it happens to be open during the time you plan to be on Staten Island, it is a great addition or substitution.

Where it Goes: Day 4.

The Jacques Marchais Museum of Tibetan Art is a unique experience nestled within the borders of Staten Island. This museum will provide your family a chance to explore art and foreign culture, while enjoying an idyllic and tranquil setting, which will result in both an educational and meditative experience. In addition to the museum, you can enjoy the edenic "Samadhi Garden", replete with a fish and lotus pond, meditation cells, and many original plantings from the turn of the

20th century. The museum was actually praised for its authenticity by the Dalai Lama, who visited in 1991.

Founded in 1945, the museum in residential Lighthouse Hill, Staten Island was founded by Jacques Marchais (1887-1948). This boundary-breaking American woman worked in the field of Tibetan Art, serving as an importer/exporter and an academic expert publishing multiple works on the subjects of Tibet and life in the Himalayas. Marchais actually designed the facility herself, hoping to create a location that resembled a Tibetan monastery. The setting adds to the exhibits, to form a complete experience which allows your family to explore the cultural heritage of Tibet, learn about its fascinating people, and step outside the city noise and into a tranquil oasis.

Fun Facts: This is the first example of Himalayan-style architecture built in the United States, and the first museum devoted solely to Tibetan art in the world.

Besides the cultural opportunities, the education, and the relaxing feel of the setting - part of the fun of this museum comes from discovering it. A hidden gem of Staten Island, this is one of those locations than many native New Yorkers don't even know about, and the location's often overlooked beauty makes it that much more special an experience for your family. Guided tours can be arranged by e-mailing for details and to make a reservation. Even if you don't arrange a tour, you will likely get hands-on treatment from the knowledgeable staff.

Travel Tip: Check the events calendar to see if anything coincides with your trip. The museum frequently offers tai chi and meditation classes, as well as films, musical performances, lectures, travel talks, traditional Tibetan crafts, and fun activities for families.

On your way in or out, make sure to take time to look past the museum grounds and enjoy the view. Lighthouse Hill offers some of the most sweeping and beautiful views of Staten Island and the surrounding area, offering you and your family a chance to really mark your time in the borough and enjoy exploring New York City off the beaten path.

Address: 338 Lighthouse Ave, Staten Island, NY 10306

Phone: (718) 987-3500

Email: info@tibetanmuseum.org

Hours: Wednesday - Sunday, 1 PM - 5 PM. Closed Monday and Tuesday.

Website: www.tibetanmuseum.org/

Approximate Cost: Adults, $6. Students and Children $4.

Approximate Length: We recommend spending about **an hour** here.

Staten Island Zoo

Why We Omitted It: We opted for the bigger and more famous Bronx Zoo as part of our main itinerary. If you and your family skip that stop, dislike our ideas for Staten Island, or simply want to pack in as much zoo time as possible, this is a great substitution.

Where it Goes: Day 4.

The Staten Island Zoo is a true family destination, catering specifically to the needs of children and committed to making family time fun and rewarding for all. The zoo has free weekend programs, numerous special events, and educational programs for children and adults. Check their calendar to see exactly what is going on at a given moment.

Interestingly enough, the zoo can trace its history back to three war heroes: Colonel Edward Harden, Colonel Richard Penn Smith, and Major Clarence Barrett. In the 19th century, Staten Island represented desirable land on which one could build a large estate. Harden and Penn Smith, heroes of the Spanish-American War and Civil War respectively, lived across from each other and their land would eventually form the main area of the zoo and its parking lot; with the combined donation borrowing its name from brother-in-law to Mrs. Harden and Civil War hero Major Barrett.

The Staten Island Zoo opened its gates in 1936 and ever since it has been dedicated to entertaining and educating residents of the island and its visitors. There are major renovations going on since 2010, with planned additions of a new carousel and an outdoor Amur leopard enclosure, expected to be one of the largest leopard enclosures in the United States.

Travel Tip: Visit on Wednesdays between 2 PM and close (4:45 PM) to enjoy FREE admission for the entire family.

The zoo features a picnic area to enjoy a nice lunch in the sun in between visiting the animals, as well as a Zoo Café for those who choose not to bring their own food. You can download a map of the zoo on their website in advance of your trip, to see what displays they have and plot a route for your time here. Enjoy everything from ostriches to otters, cassowaries to horses, at this zoological monument to family fun.

Address: 614 Broadway, Staten Island, NY 10310

Phone: (718) 442-3100

Hours: Daily, 10 AM - 4:45 PM.

Website: www.statenislandzoo.org/

Approximate Cost: Adults (15 and older), $8. Children (3-14), $5. Children 2 and under FREE.

Approximate Length: We recommend about **1-3 hours here**, depending on how much of the rest of the day you are willing to substitute.

Alice Austen House Museum and Garden

Why We Omitted It: The limited scope of the material here makes it a more specialized choice than the general interest activities of the main itinerary. If this is a particularly interesting subject for your family, we think it makes a great substitution.

Where it Goes: Day 4.

Also known by the house's name, Clear Comfort, the Alice Austen House Museum and its accompanying garden honors one of America's great women in an immersive setting. Alice Austen was one of America's most prolific photographers and an instrumental figure in gaining ground for women in the arts. The Dutch Colonial house, which served as her home and studio, was opened to the public in 1985. It is situated on the eastern shore of Staten Island, overlooking The Narrows and the Verrazano-Narrows Bridge.

Originally built in the 1690's, this is one of the oldest homes in all of New York City, and the location provides an opportunity to delve into both the history of life in New York, and the famous woman who lived here. Families are welcome to enjoy a self-guided tour on their own, taking in exhibitions and enjoying the natural setting of the home, or group tours can be booked in advance (contact the home by phone or email to arrange one).

The house reflects the Victorian middle class values of the 19th century. The carefully tended home and gardens, as well as the family's art collection, would influence the photography that took the world by storm. Originally built as a one room cottage, the home was later expanded to its current size. In this way, it also represents the growth of New York City homes during this time period, and the constant evolution of Staten Island's landscape.

Austen's photography was groundbreaking, representing one of the first opportunities by a woman to work outside of a studio as she wielded her camera freely in the world at large. The development of her own personal style of documentary photography was ahead of her time, influenced other photographers, and helped give birth to the industry of photojournalism some 40 years later.

The house's collection of Austen photography is unmatched, and the chance to see the woman's work and home life side by side offers a unique insight into her development and process. Whether you come during a special event or just pop in for an hour or so and look around, there is something for every member of the family here as a fascinating bit of American culture plays out before your eyes.

Address: 2 Hylan Blvd, Staten Island, NY 10305

Phone: (718) 816-4506 ext. 10

Email: info@aliceausten.org

Hours: Tuesday - Sunday, 11 AM - 5 PM. Closed Mondays. Grounds open every day until dusk.

Website: http://aliceausten.org/

Approximate Cost: $3 suggested donation.

Approximate Length: We recommend about **an hour** here.

Queens

Museum of the Moving Image

Why We Omitted It: Queens has a number of quality museums. We simply made choices we believed would appeal to most families. If you find the subject matter here more interesting than our options, swap it in for a day that caters to your family best.

Where it Goes: Day 6.

NOTE: With a dedication to film education, half the fun here is the screenings of great movies. Many screenings take place in the evening. See the calendar for screening times, and consider leaving this stop for the end of the day so you can round out the evening with family movie time after touring the museum.

Located in the home building of the Kaufman Astoria Studios in Queens, this museum, dedicated to film as art and the history of moving pictures is a fascinating take on this modern form and its contribution to our culture. The facility catalogs everything from actual films, to film equipment, and movie artifacts. The museum's collection provides a comprehensive look at the art, history, technique, and technology of film, television, and digital media.

As you would expect, audio/visual components, film clips, and other media viewed on a plethora of screens make up the bulk of the experience here. At the same time, don't expect to simply spend your entire time watching. The film artifacts are a fascinating component that lend context to the process of film creation, and offer children a unique insight into how their favorite movies and television programs get made.

Exhibits like "Behind the Screen" - which immerses visitors in the technical processes of making and displaying a piece of film - also include interactive components to keep children interested. Record your child's movements on museum equipment, then print them out as a flip book you can take home. You can also create stop-motion animations and email them to yourself for posterity; record voices over dialogue from a film, just like actors dubbing their lines in post-production; and play around with changing the tone or feel of a scene in a movie by adding music and sound effects.

Fun Fact: Children will also be excited to know that the museum holds one of the largest and most comprehensive collections of video games and gaming hardware in the world.

The subject matter here lends itself to family exploration, as media forms a regular and important part of life and recreation for so many families. This museum provides an educational experience in a special way that allows families to come together and enjoy a memory they can all share. Let kids learn about the Muppets while parents enjoy a behind the scenes look at *Mad Men* - examples of just two of the exciting exhibits the museum has put on in recent years/will soon.

The museum has a strong commitment to family fun, and drop-in studio sessions most Saturdays (included with museum admission) allow children ages 7 and up to enjoy and engage in hands-on creative work. Play with the technology that helps create movies and videogames, for a special interactive experience. Holiday weekends also see a host of family workshops. See the upcoming events page of their website for details.

Address: 36-01 35th Ave, New York, NY 11106 (Astoria, Queens)

Phone: (718) 777-6800

Hours: Wednesday and Thursday, 10:30 AM - 5 PM. Friday, 10:30 AM - 8 PM. Saturday and Sunday, 10:30 AM - 7 PM. Closed Mondays and Tuesdays. See calendar for screening times.

Website: www.movingimage.us/

Approximate Cost: General Admission - Adults, $12. Students, $9. Children (3-12), $6.

PLEASE NOTE: Tickets are required for most screenings, at the same prices as above, and these generally include museum admission. In other words, if you plan on seeing a screening, buy that ticket first and use it as your museum entrance ticket as well.

Approximate Length: We recommend about an **hour and a half to two hours** here, unless you plan on seeing a screening, in which case you may spend several hours here between touring and the film.

Fort Totten

Why We Omitted It: Our day in Queens calls for more educational experiences in the form of museums, and some time for relaxing/playing in the larger Corona Park. If you want to skip a museum for more park time, or enjoy some sightseeing rather than activity time, this is a great substitution.

Where it Goes: Day 6.

This former US Army base lies at the head of Little Neck Bay, the spot where the East River gives way to the Long Island Sound. It represents one extreme tip of New York City, on a peninsula that offers lovely views of the surrounding area, as well as the unique opportunity to tour a (semi) active US Army base.

Urban Park Rangers lead regular tours of the fortress and the wildlife surrounding it, which are perfect for families who want to learn as much as they can about the area. The park's visitors' center is great for those who want to go it on their own, as you can find information to create a self-guided tour.

Fun Fact: Shortly after the Federal Government announced intentions to close Fort Totten, The Queens Tribune ran a story in their annual April Fool's Day issue. It announced that the Disney Corporation had purchased Fort Totten and was planning a new super theme park called "Fort Disney." Many homes were immediately put on the market by outraged locals, who calmed down after the hoax was revealed.

Of course, you can choose to forgo the touring and just take the chance to relax in a delightful Queens park. Besides opportunities to explore the fortress and surrounding buildings, each season offers unique opportunities for families. In the fall, a special haunted house makes an appearance at the old water battery. The winter offers chances for birdwatching, at a spot famous as a stopover for birds migrating south for the colder months. Spring and summer offer chances to take a canoe out into the Long Island Sound, or just relax and sun in between dips in the pool.

Historic Fort Totten was completed in 1863, with initial plans proposed by then Captain Robert E. Lee. It originally offered artillery support that defended New York Harbor and provided integral long-range support during the Civil War. As the technology that was installed here became outdated, the fort eventually transitioned to hospital care and fell out of more active use. The US Army still maintains a small presence here, out of the way of public areas. Occasionally, Urban Rangers offer guided tours of the normally inaccessible tunnels of the fort, for a look at where munitions were housed and transported.

Address: 422 Weaver Ave, Bayside, NY 11359

Phone: (718) 352-4793

Hours: Daily, 11 AM - 7 PM. Hours vary for activities and pool.

Website: www.nycgovparks.org/parks/fort-totten-park

Approximate Cost: FREE of charge.

Approximate Length: We recommend **1-2 hours** here.

Belmont Park and Race Track

Why We Omitted It: Horse racing isn't for everyone, and the seasonal nature also makes it hard for us to recommend this site for a main itinerary. Also, since it is technically located in Elmont, New York, we felt best to leave it out of our New York City itinerary.

Where it Goes: Day 6.

While technically just outside the New York City limits, this racetrack is a New York institution, and a major part of city history. This is the site of the annual Belmont Stakes, the third leg of horse racing's "Triple Crown" and the world renowned "Test of the Champion." Whether you come to see a race, just walk the grounds to take in the vibe, or participate in a special event, Belmont is a great space to show your children as you admire some of the finest examples from the "sport of kings" - just outside of Queens.

While horse racing may have fallen out of national favor to some degree, with many only tuning in for the three biggest races of the year (one of which takes place at this track), in the earlier days of New York City, this track and the sport of horse racing were important parts of the culture. This was a place where the wealthiest citizens (often owning the horses) could come together with the working class to enjoy the same attraction side by side.

Racing at Belmont Park is conducted in two annual installments, or "meetings": The "spring-summer meeting," which usually begins partway through May and lasts through the end of July, followed by a "fall meeting" opening on the Friday after Labor Day and finishing at the end of October. In between these periods, races take place at other tracks. If you and your family will be in town during a "meeting" see the Belmont website for a schedule of races and come show your kids these powerful animals in action.

Travel Tip: Belmont Park offers "family fun days" on certain Sundays. The backyard picnic area is filled with food and fun activities for families to enjoy together.

If you want to keep your time here short, if everyone is feeling a little too restless for the stands, or you simply want to enjoy the races in a different way - check out the backyard area of the track. There is open space for food and picnicking, a playground for children, and concessions stands for food and drink. The races are displayed on TVs so you can still catch some of the action, while enjoying a park-like atmosphere just behind the main facility.

With general admission tickets you are free to explore the track, watch as many races as you like, and take in historical displays that teach you about the story of Belmont and the men and women who made it great. Take in the fun atmosphere and enjoy the special opportunity to see some of the best horses in the world at a venue that has been providing family fun throughout the history of New York City.

Address: 2150 Hempstead Turnpike, Elmont, NY 11003

Phone: (718) 641-4700

Hours: Wednesday - Sunday, 11:30 AM - 5 PM.

Website: www.nyra.com/belmont/

Approximate Cost: General admission is $5 per person.

Approximate Length: Walking around and exploring could take an **hour** or less. Staying for races or an event increases that time, though there is some flexibility for you to choose how long you want to stay.

SUMMER - Beach Time at Jacob Riis Park

Why We Omitted It: While there are things to do in the park year round, the real draw is the chance to enjoy the beach and hop in the water, which really only makes sense in the summer. We left it off the main itinerary for families travelling in colder months, but it makes a great substitution/addition if your trip coincides with the warm weather. **PLEASE NOTE**: We do offer time at the beach in the main itinerary, as part of the Coney Island Stop on Day 3 in Brooklyn.

Where it Goes: Day 6.

Part of the Gateway National Recreation Area, operated by the National Parks department, this area of Jamaica Bay has a lot to offer families. A famous Art Deco bath house sits beside seaside recreation areas, and some of New York City's best surf, sand, and beach areas.

For year-round visits, the national landmark of a bathhouse also serves as an information center, where ranger-led tours and information sessions cover the history of the park and the surrounding area. There are also a miniature golf facility, food, and sport facilities that operate in all seasons.

As we mentioned, the real draw here is the beach. Following a traditional Memorial Day - Labor Day opening schedule, here you will find a wheelchair accessible boardwalk full of activities for families. The beach itself is great for sunning, picnicking, paddleball, and volleyball. Swim and sunbathe on a clean and well-kept beach just miles from the tall buildings and concrete jungle of Manhattan.

Named for Jacob Riis, the famous muckraker journalist and photographer, the park pays homage to a man who documented the plight of the poor and working class in New York City. Enjoy the opportunity to sunbathe alongside locals and indulge in a little of the fun that native citizens favor for their own downtime.

Travel Tip: As the beach here does serve primarily as an escape for locals, it is busiest on the weekends when locals are not working. Visiting on a weekday will afford you more space to spread out and help avoid the crowds.

Check the calendar online for a list of special events that may coincide with your visit. Saddle up alongside locals as you enjoy swimming, sandcastle building, and a chance to search for endangered piping plovers at a site that marries the best of a national park with a public beach.

Address: 157 Rockaway Beach Blvd, Rockaway Park, NY 11694

Phone: (718) 318-4300

Hours: Generally open from sunrise to sunset, though this may vary with certain times of year and certain areas may close at different times.

Website: www.nps.gov/gate/index.htm

Approximate Cost: FREE of Charge.

Approximate Length: We recommend limiting time here to about **2 hours** in order not to sacrifice too many other opportunities in Queens, however, if your family just wants to take a "beach day the choice is yours.

Appendix B: Resources at RealFamilyTrips.com

For those readers looking for even more ideas, great connections, and more detailed background information, we recommend visiting us online. Part of our goal in this book has been to provide you with a great vacation, the other part has been about empowering you to make choices and become experts. We want you and your children to arrive in the country already knowing how much fun you are about to have, and we hope that our resources will help allay any flagging concerns, and help you get that much more excited.

The articles on our site represent great itineraries (some for New York City and the surrounding area), guides to common travel problems, and ways to save money for you and your children as you plan your trip. Take the time to browse them at your leisure. They may contain other ideas not in these pages that change your plans. They may help confirm that you have made the right choices for your family. They may simply provide more material for you to read in the days leading up to your arrival in New York City, to help raise excitement and get you all prepared for the coming fun.

Some of the information on the site leant ideas for the book, and some of the book will eventually lend itself to new content online. By purchasing this book you are now part of our family, and as such, you should enjoy all that we have learned and continue to enjoy sharing.

About the Resources on RealFamilyTrips.com

The website that put this book together, we host a variety of useful information to supplement that in these pages and further help you plan a great trip.

- Our section of **Travel Tips** provides articles on a wide variety of topics, many useful for the vacation outlined in this book. You will find information on purchasing souvenirs, taking photos, and reviews of great travel apps - and that is just the beginning. These articles will help you cover both the basics and the extras as you plan a fun a rewarding vacation.
- Our **Itineraries Section** contains days in cities all over the world, much like those you have enjoyed in this book. You will find several for New York City, as well as some for areas in New Jersey, New York State, and the surrounding New York Metropolitan Area - in case you are interested in expanding your trip to explore further, or if you live in the area and want other ideas for close-to-home excursions.
- Our **Spotlight Articles** feature in-depth information on great locations, topics of interest, and types of vacations. Often, they combine multiple itineraries on a single theme to help find commonalities and inspire you to choose destinations you might not otherwise have thought of. Be sure to check out our Broadway related spotlight piece, previously mentioned in this book.

Also be sure to check out our previous book, Israel for Families: An Adventure in 12 Days

Much like this volume, it includes an expansive and exciting itinerary (lasting 12 touring days) and covers the entire nation of Israel from north to south. The days include a mix of active pursuits and cultural explorations in one of the most storied lands on earth. You will also find all the same great features like advice on enjoying your trip, alternate activities, additional resources, and original fiction for children.

Be on the lookout for other great books in the future, with the latest updates on our site.

The Team at RealFamilyTrips.com

Who Helped Put This Book Together

Our team works tirelessly to bring you the best in travel information and writing, from one real family to countless others. Get to know the group at RealFamilyTrips.com and what makes us different from other family travel resources.

Noah Greenblatt

Noah is 16 years old and just finished his sophomore year in high school. He takes his studies seriously, and loves science. His hobbies include skiing, basketball, baseball, and of course, travel. Noah enjoys hanging out with friends and family. Noah loves time spent vacationing with family and all it has taught him.

Julia Greenblatt

Julia is also a sixteen year old high school student who just completed her sophomore year. She enjoys playing soccer and drawing. In her free time, she volunteers for The Friendship Circle, something she loves to do. Julia's favorite subject is history, and she loves learning about different cultures and civilizations. Julia enjoys the opportunities travelling with family affords her to learn firsthand about the world around her.

Anna Greenblatt

Anna is also a 16 year old who just finished her sophomore year in high school (see a pattern?). She enjoys playing soccer, drawing, reading, and hanging out with her family and friends. Anna is very enthusiastic about helping to make the world a better place through her involvement in charity work, and the chance to see the world through travel helps motivate this passion for service.

Sophia Greenblatt

Sophia just completed 6th grade. She loves ice skating and soccer. Sophia's favorite subject is English. Sophia is excited to share about vacationing with her family and looks forward to time spent with her parents and siblings when they go away together.

Avery Greenblatt

Avery is 9 years old. He just completed 3rd Grade. His favorite hobbies are playing basketball and football. He also loves learning math in school. He enjoys the time that he spends with his family. He is excited to have joined the team at RealFamilyTrips.com and hopes to have a great impact on the site and its goals.

Vera Greenblatt

Vera is a four year old girl (going on 16!) who loves to have fun. She enjoys doing ballet and playing with her siblings. When Vera grows up she wants to be just like her mom! She is the newest member of RealFamilyTrips.com and we look forward to seeing what she can do!

Naomi Greenblatt

Dr. Naomi Greenblatt is an NYU educated psychiatrist who maintains a private practice in reproductive psychiatry. Dr. Greenblatt is a diplomate of the American Board of Psychiatry. She is a frequent lecturer and has been featured on the radio as well as in numerous publications. She is proud to be a co-founder of RealFamilyTrips.com and hopes to help other families achieve the sort of meaningful growth through travel that she has enjoyed with her family.

Jason Greenblatt

Jason Greenblatt Esq is a well-known real estate attorney. In addition to his successful career in law, he is an accomplished public speaker and an adjunct professor who teaches about real estate. As a co-founder of RealFamilyTrips.com, Jason recognizes travel as an important part of his treasured family time, as well as a powerful tool for growth and education.

Ryan Kagy

Ryan is the Head Writer at RealFamilyTrips.com. Born to a family that valued and celebrated travel, he has known and enjoyed the benefits of a good trip from a young age. He is proud to lead content generation for RealFamilyTrips.com, this volume, and InspireConversation.com. He would like to thank Laura and his parents for their continued love, inspiration, and support in his life.

The "Fine Print"

This book is provided without any guarantees or warranties of any kind, express or implied. Your use of the book, and the services and vendors mentioned, is at your sole risk. Real Family Trips, Inspire Conversation LLC and each of their members, shareholders, partners, owners and affiliates (all of the foregoing, collectively, the "Publisher and Related Parties") will not be held responsible for any damages of any type due to your use of the book or services and vendors mentioned.

Although Real Family Trips has made every effort to ensure that the information in this book was correct at press time, the author and publisher do not assume and hereby disclaim any liability to anyone for any loss, damage, or disruption caused by errors or omissions, whether such errors or omissions result from negligence, accident, or any other cause.

All information provided in this book is intended for informational and entertainment purposes only. The views expressed are personal opinions only. Neither Real Family Trips nor its parent company Inspire Conversation LLC is responsible for any legal, medical, financial, or other hardships caused by acting on the information provided in this book. Unless otherwise noted, all material in the book is the legal property of Real Family Trips and/or Inspire Conversation LLC and may not be reprinted or republished without the express written consent of Real Family Trips and/or Inspire Conversation LLC. When applicable, every attempt has been made to correctly credit the legal owners of photos and other various media. Please contact us if you feel that you have not been credited properly.

Your use of the book constitutes your agreement and acknowledgment that you hold the Publisher and Related Parties harmless and understand that the Publisher and Related Parties are not liable in any way for any claims, causes of action, liability, damage, or other actions or obligations that may arise from your use of the book or any products, vendors or services contained therein.

Image Credits

We thank all those who contributed photos and images to help bring New York City to life for this book.

Cover - Assembled and Designed by Derek Aubie

Photos (clockwise from the top left)

- Brooklyn Bridge, Dave Newman © 123RF.com
- Manhattan Skyline, jovannig © 123RF.com
- Wall Street Sign, Steve Collender © 123RF.com
- Statue of Liberty, Erich Teister © 123RF.com

Introduction - Statue of Liberty on NYC Skyline, upthebanner © 123RF.com

Day 1

- American Museum of Natural History, Shane Saunders © 123RF.com
- Aerial Photo of Central Park, Francois Roux © 123RF.com
- SWTL Overview Shot, Photo Courtesy of Sony Wonder Technology Lab

Day 2

- Polar Bear at the Bronx Zoo, Gordon Donovan © 123RF.com
- The Enid A. Haupt Conservatory at the New York Botanical Garden, Jack Aiello © 123RF.com
- Aerial View of The Bronx from Manhattan, konstantin32 © 123RF.com

Day 3

- Parachute Jump at Coney Island, Victoria Lipov © 123RF.com
- Bicylces on the Brooklyn Promenade, andreka © 123RF.com
- Sunset Over the Brooklyn Bridge, jovannig © 123RF.com

Day 4

- Staten Island Ferry, Richard Semik © 123RF.com
- Chinese Scholar's Garden at Snug Harbor, Photo © RealFamilyTrips.com
- Sculpture at Lenny's Creations, Photo © RealFamilyTrips.com

Day 5

- Pier A in Battery Park, Tono Balaguer © 123RF.com
- Wall Street Sign, Steve Collender © 123RF.com
- Washington Arch in Greenwich Village, tupungato © 123RF.com

Day 6

- Aerial View of Queens, Dereje Belachew © 123RF.com
- View of Queens and Queensboro Bridge from Roosevelt Island, Felix Lipov © 123RF.com
- The Unisphere at Corona Park, Paul Hakimata © 123RF.com

Day 7

- Times Square, dibrova © 123RF.com
- Bryant Park, jovannig © 123RF.com
- The Beast - Photo Courtesy of Circle Line Sightseeing Cruises

Story Part I

- Horse and Buggy in Central Park, Andrew Kazmierski © 123RF.com

Story Part II
- Vintage Green Leaves, weedezign © 123RF.com

Story Part III
- Redcoat Playing a Drum, odessa4 © 123RF.com

Story Part IV
- George Washington Statue at Federal Hall, Sean Pavone © 123RF.com

Story Part V
- Closeup of US Quarter, Vitaliy Kytayko © 123RF.com

Alternates - Manhattan
- Manhattan Skyline at Dusk, Harold Stiver © 123RF.com

Alternates - The Bronx
- Van Cortlandt Park, Eddie Toro © 123RF.com

Alternates - Brooklyn
- Brooklyn Harbor, Markus Gann © 123RF.com

Alternates - Staten Island
- Whitehall Terminal in Staten Island, Juan G. Auninn © 123RF.com

Alternates - Queens
- Racing at Belmont, Ashok Padmanabhan © 123RF.com

www.ingramcontent.com/pod-product-compliance
Lightning Source LLC
Chambersburg PA
CBHW071912290426
44110CB00013B/1362